The Brady Bunch
super groovy after all these years!

By Mike Pingel
Foreword by Charlene Tilton

The Brady Bunch: Super Groovy After All These Years!
© 2010 Mike Pingel. All Rights Reserved.

All illustrations are copyright of their respective owners, and are also reproduced here in the spirit of publicity. Whilst we have made every effort to acknowledge specific credits whenever possible, we apologize for any omissions, and will undertake every effort to make any appropriate changes in future editions of this book if necessary.

No part of this book may be reproduced in any form or by any means, electronic, mechanical, digital, photocopying or recording, except for the inclusion in a review, without permission in writing from the publisher.

Published in the USA by:
BearManor Media
P O Box 71426
Albany, Georgia 31708
www.bearmanormedia.com

ISBN 1-59393-466-1

Printed in the United States of America.

Book design by Darlene Swanson of Van-garde Imagery, Inc.
Illustration by artist: Michael Derry www.derryproducts.com
Book cover design by: Danielle Buerli, ArtMachine

contents

	Foreword by Charlene Tilton vii
Chapter One:	A Groovy Brady Story 1
	A Brady Chat with Sherwood Schwartz
Chapter Two:	The Brady Actors. 23
	A Brady Chat with Susan Olsen
	A Brady Chat with Ann B. Davis
Chapter Three:	A Brady Chat with Lloyd Schwartz 41
	Brady Books
Chapter Four:	Bradys Reincarnated 57
	A Brady Chat with Geri Reischl
	The Second Bradys
	A Brady Chat with Zach Bostrom
	A Brady Chat with Hope Juber
Chapter Five	Brady TV Effect. 81
	Why We Love The Bradys
	A Brady Chat with Wendy Winans

Chapter Six:	The Very Brady Characters 89	
	A Brady Chat with Robbie Rist "Cousin Oliver"	
Chapter Seven:	The Brady Episode Stories 101	
	Season One	
	Season Two	
	Season Three	
	Season Four	
	The Brady Toy Chest & Record Set	

Bibliography 173

Acknowledgements 175

About the Author 179

I dedicate this book to my sister Elizabeth, her husband Rob and their very own Brady Bunch, my ultra cool nephews Jamison and Kendrick.

Author Mike Pingel with Brady Bunch creator and producer Sherwood Schwartz in 2008. (photo © Mike Pingel)

A Very Brady Foreword

Just like the Bradys, I, too, was a part of a TV family that loved all the way down to the core - but we lived in Dallas! As Lucy Ewing, I was the youngest of our bunch. Lucy easily could have been a Brady. She was the all-American girl who never got in trouble, never rolled around in the hay or ever told a lie (wink-wink)! All right, you got me. We know that Lucy and the whole Ewing clan were about as far from being a wholesome white-picket-fence family as they could be.

I must admit that I still hold the Brady Bunch close to my heart. As a young girl my family didn't have much money and couldn't even afford a TV set. I would take the bus down to the Sears, go into their TV display room and watch the show.

Throughout my career I have been able to work with many of the Brady Kids and they are just as cool and fun as they were on TV!

As you stroll down the Brady memory lane I'm sure you will be as taken as I have been with these super-groovy pages which are dedicated to that all-American family that we all wanted to be a part of (... and still do). They are an American institution. Long live the Bradys!

Charlene Tilton

The Brady Bunch cast with show creator, writer and producer Sherwood Schwartz in the 1970s. (Image courtesy of Sherwood Schwartz)

Chapter one!

A Very Brady History Lesson

It was 1965. TV producer Sherwood Schwartz was reading the paper and came up with a clever idea. Who would have thought that this simple act would begin the world-wide love affair with a family that became as American as Apple pie and baseball?

Schwartz had already made a name for himself in TV. He had worked as a script consultant on *My Favorite Martian* and had written scripts for *I Married Joan*, *The Red Skelton Show* and *Mr. and Mrs.* (also called *The Lucille Ball Comedy Hour*). He pitched a show about six stranded castaways called *Gilligan's Island* in 1961, which made audiences laugh on CBS from 1964-1967.

One day, while reading the *Los Angeles Times*, Schwartz spotted a small article that mentioned that 29% of all the new marriages formed a new type of family. New couples were getting remarried and merging their kids from their first marriages. He thought this would be a great base for a new series called *Yours & Mine*, which would center on this new family component. His original idea for the show was about a woman divorcee who marries a man who has lost his wife. Each parent came into the marriage with three children and the show would focus on the kids' problems. These issues were to be taken very seriously, such as getting braces, wearing glasses, school bullies, lying, dating, and a first kiss. Thinking that someone else was sure to have the same idea, Schwartz immediately wrote up his idea and took it to the Writers Guild of America to have it copyrighted.

He made the rounds to the Hollywood TV networks to sell his new show idea. The networks were interested, but they all wanted to tweak the idea. Schwartz didn't want to change his initial idea, so he ended up shelving it.

A couple years later, in 1968, Paramount Pictures produced a new theatrical film, *Yours, Mine & Ours*, which starred comedic icon Lucille Ball and Henry Fonda. The storyline was about two widows who remarry and combine their eighteen kids. The similarity of the feature film was very close to Schwartz's registered idea.

Executives at ABC-TV remembered Schwartz's pitch for *Yours & Mine* and green-lit his series. This would become Paramount Pictures' very first TV series. Up to that point, the studio had only made feature films.

The studio did make some minor changes to the plot. For the time period, they thought the idea of Carol being divorced was too taboo. During the series' entire run, neither Carol's divorce, nor her ex-husband's name were ever mentioned. And Mike's deceased wife was never mention either, although her photo is seen in the pilot episode.

groovy tip!

The film *Yours, Mine & Ours* was remade in 2005 with Rene Russo and Dennis Quaid and brought in $53 million dollars at the box office.

groovy tip!

Christopher Knight, who played Peter Brady, was the only kid who had brown eyes, all the others had blue.

Mixing the Bradys

With the series idea finding its home, the next step was to cast the Brady kids. This was quite a task for Schwartz; he interviewed hundreds of kids for the six parts. During the auditions, he had placed toys on a desk for the kids to play with. If the kids were more interested in playing with the toys, he felt that they would not be ready to work on the series.

Not knowing who was to be cast as the TV parents, Schwartz chose two sets of kids, one set all having blonde hair, the other set with brunette hair.

The only kid that he knew right off the bat that he wanted to cast was the spunky Susan Olsen, who become the unforgettable Cindy Brady. Olsen had just had a birthday and the production office sang "Happy Birthday" to her. At that moment, Olsen knew she wanted to work with them.

Mike Lookinland was the last Brady kid to be cast. He had auditioned early on but was passed over because he had red hair. The casting department continued their nationwide search and was ready to cast another child actor, but they had really liked Lookinland and asked him if he would be willing to dye his hair for the part of Bobby Brady. He accepted the job not knowing the show would go on for five years.

The audition for the show included two interviews and a screen test to see how the kids looked on film.

The original choices for Carol and Mike Brady were Florence Henderson and Gene Hackman. However, Henderson was off on a singing tour and was unavailable. Funny lady Joyce Bulifant was then hired for the role, but her agent sat on the paperwork. In the interim, Henderson returned back to Los Angeles from her tour and auditioned for the role. Paramount and Schwartz ended up going with their first choice.

groovy tip!

Joyce Bulifant went on to be a semi-regular on *Dr. Kildare* and *The Bill Cosby Show* (1969). She is best known as Marie, the wife to Murray Slaughter, on *The Mary Tyler Moore Show*.

At the time, Gene Hackman had a budding career, with numerous films and TV appearances, including *Bonnie and Clyde* and *The Gypsy Moths*; he had even appeared in three episodes of Robert Reed's series, *The Defenders*. The studio felt that Hackman was too green for the role of Mike Brady, so they passed on casting him.

groovy tip!

In 1968, Gene Hackman was nominated for his first Oscar, for his role in *Bonnie and Clyde* (1967). He went on to become one of Hollywood's leading men, with two Oscar wins, Best Actor for *The French Connection* (1971) and Supporting Actor for *Unforgiven* (1992).

In a turn of events, Robert Reed, who was known for his work in the TV series *The Defenders* and *Dr. Kildare*, had signed with Paramount to do a new series based on two feature films, but, as fate would have it, neither series were produced. Paramount sent Reed Schwartz's way and all involved thought he would be perfect as Mike Brady.

With the parents' roles cast, the kids were next. The blonde Brady girls were selected, with Maureen McCormick as the sweetheart Marcia, Eve Plumb as the middle child Jan and Susan Olsen as the youngest one in curls, Cindy.

On the father's side, the brunette boys selected were Barry Williams as Greg the oldest child, Christopher Knight as the middle brother Peter, and Mike Lookinland as Bobby the youngest son.

As for the role of Alice the family housekeeper, actress Monty Margetts was originally cast. After hiring Florence Henderson, Schwartz decided to recast the housekeeper and have her be a funny lady in the kitchen. In came Ann B. Davis, who had won two Emmy awards and was known as one of entertainment's funny ladies.

Schwartz wanted to change the title of the show from *Yours & Mine* to *The Brady Bunch*. However, the network thought that the word "Bunch" was too racy. At the time, the word "bunch" had many bad connotations linked to it, so the title was changed to *The Brady Brood*. Schwartz fought for *The Brady Bunch*, and the final change was made before it hit the airwaves.

Schwartz hired director John Rich, who worked on his shows *I Married Joan* and *Gilligan's Island*, to take the helm of directing the pilot. Rich had a tough task ahead of him, not only creating the world of the Bradys, but working with a cat and a dog; it took three hours to get the cat to jump over the ladies' laps.

The pilot took three weeks to film between the interior and exterior sets. The outdoor scenes were filmed in the Valley, about 20 miles away from the Paramount Pictures lot.

During the pilot, the producers got their first glimpse of Robert Reed's fight for better scripts as he informed Sherwood Schwartz that he should save the "cake in the face" for his other show, *Gilligan's Island*. It was over the comic scenes that Reed came to blows with the producers, but he was right on target for the dramatic scenes.

The series was quickly picked up after the pilot was filmed, and was placed on the ABC fall schedule for Friday nights at 8:00 p.m.

From the beginning, TV critics were not fans of the show. Even *TV Guide's* Fall Preview of 1968, which gave a full-page description and photo for each new fall show, barely showcased *The Brady Bunch* in the issue.

groovy tip!

In 1979, Florence Henderson, Robert Reed, Maureen McCormick, Christopher Knight and Susan Olsen appeared in the celebrity edition of the TV game show *Family Feud*.

As the season began, each kid's character began to become very distinct. Although the characters were not patterned after the actors, they did try to match their characters' way of speaking into how the actor would recite their lines. Their efforts didn't always work. Susan Olsen, who played Cindy, was not always happy with the way her character was portrayed. She felt they wrote Cindy as being stupid, which was far from how Olsen was in real life.

The writing did manage to find the "heart" of *The Brady Bunch*. It was more than just a family comedy, but it was written with intelligence and seriousness, which gave the show a more realistic family outlook.

From the beginning, Brady father figure Robert Reed wanted out of his contract. He constantly fought against Schwartz about poor scripts and would send long notes with his thoughts for changes with certain episodes. However, Reed always made sure not to come to blows with Schwartz in front of the kids. Sherwood recalls that Florence Henderson was always a trouper, and she would help out by taking Reed's lines if he didn't want to do them.

groovy tip!

First Lady Michele Obama, the wife of the 44th President Barack H. Obama, was "outed" by her brother at the 2008 Democratic convention. It's true! Mrs. Obama is an avid fan of *The Brady Bunch*. As a kid, she would watch and memorize all the lines of each episode. Can we say, "Michele! Michele! Michele!"

Through the seasons:

Beginning in the second season, the Brady kids started to branch out into music by singing the series' theme song. This snowballed into the idea of having the kids record an album, especially since *The Partridge Family*, which followed *The Brady Bunch* Friday nights on ABC, had released a record album that was very successful.

The Brady kids were shipped into the studio to crank out their first album, *Merry Christmas from the Brady Bunch*, within two weeks. In the next few years they would release four more albums, *Meet the Bradys, The Kids from the Brady Bunch, Brady Bunch Phonographic Album,* and *Chris Knight and Maureen McCormick* (which featured Maureen and Chris only). The show incorporated these songs into the storylines to help promote the albums. They also did a concert tour in 1972, sharing the stage with Tony Orlando and Dawn and The Fifth Dimension.

As the show went into the fourth season, there was a huge transformation in the Brady boys' hair. As they prepared to leave for Hawaii from Los Angeles, their hair was straight. Upon arriving in Hawaii, Robert Reed, Barry Williams and Christopher Knight suddenly had curly hair. From that point forward, all three sported their classic Brady perms.

While filming the episode "The Cincinnati Kids" (#106), the cast understood what it felt like to be a "Rock Star." While filming at Kings Island Amusement Park in Cincinnati, OH, they discovered that they needed security to hold back the hoards of people crowding around to take pictures and to watch them film. At one point it became very scary for them as fans tried to get into their hotel rooms.

groovy tip!

The two top 1970s American TV families were The Brady Bunch and The Partridge Family, which aired back-to-back on ABC-TV. Ironically, the cast of the Brady Bunch only met the cast of Partridge Family once, when they appeared in the Santa Claus Lane Parade in Los Angeles.

groovy tip!

When the Brady Kids received fan mail containing a fan's school picture, they would place the photo up on the wall in the schoolroom where they did their daily studies on the set.

Paramount Hijinks

Everyone wanted to be a part of the *Brady Bunch*, including Henry Kissinger, the Secretary of State. Both he and his son dropped by the set one day to see where the family lived.

The Brady Bunch was filmed on the Paramount Studios lot in Los Angeles, CA. The lot was full of activity in those days, filming shows such as *Star Trek, Mission: Impossible, The Odd Couple* and *Bonanza*.

In the early years of the show, Paramount did not allow the kids' parents to drive or park their cars onto the lot. Instead, they had to park across the street outside the studio. Eventually, they were given their own parking spaces, but the kids' names were not placed on the spaces, thinking that it would give them "inflated" egos.

As the set became a "home away from home," the kids would drive the set dresser crazy when they would move their toys and props all around the Brady house.

Barry Williams, Christopher Knight and Mike Lookinland would run around the Paramount lot playing hide-and-seek on the various sets. They even played in the condemned commissary's meat locker.

It was a true family on and off camera as the cast and their families became a tight-knit group. And Barry Williams became the "unofficial" leader of the Brady kids.

Christopher Knight was constantly poking fun at Maureen McCormick. During one episode where the boys had frogs, Christopher terrorized Maureen with them. He even told her that the "fake" braces she wore would change her teeth for good, which really upset Maureen and made her mother angry.

groovy tip!
While filming in Hawaii, two cast members had near-death experiences caught on film. Susan Olsen almost drowned after she fell overboard and could not swim. Luckily, Florence Henderson pulled her out of the water. Barry Williams nearly hit his head on a coral reef while filming his surfing scenes. These clips were not used because the network considered them to be too dangerous for a *Brady Bunch* episode.

groovy tip!
In August 2008, Barry Williams, Susan Olsen and Mike Lookinland reunited for a mini-Brady reunion at the Kings Island Amusement Park, the location where they filmed the episode "The Cincinnati Kids."

Brady friends & Lovers
On and off set, all the kids were great friends. Mike Lookinland and Susan Olsen would have sleepovers at each other's houses. When Mike was at Susan's, he would not take his eyes off their TV because in his family they were only allowed to watch *The Brady Bunch* and that was it. Maureen Mc-Cormick and Eve Plumb would hang out after work and on the weekends. Chris and Mike also spent time together outside the studio on their hobby of making and flying rockets.

groovy tip!
All six Brady kids had to share two dressing rooms during the series' entire run.

groovy tip!

The Bradys' infamous sliding glass door never had any glass in it.

At times, full-fledged hormones would put the Brady household on edge. Susan Olsen and Mike Lookinland were the first ones caught as they were making out in Tiger's doghouse. Soon after, the twosome had a fake marriage ceremony and celebrated their honeymoon during the filming of the episode "A-camping We Will Go" (#8). Sadly, their state of wedded bliss didn't live past the filming of their 22nd episode, as Mike had wandering eyes toward Eve Plumb. Eve, however, had eyes for Christopher Knight, but it wasn't reciprocated until they were on a cruise ship to England.

Barry Williams had his eyes set on Maureen McCormick from the first day of shooting. Barry and Maureen dated on and off throughout the series. Barry even had a mini-crush on his TV mom, Florence Henderson, whom he asked out. At the end of the date, he was able to sneak a very innocent kiss from her.

Brady girls Maureen and Eve flirted on the lesbian side of the Brady Astroturf! In Maureen's book, *Here's the Story*, she reveals that they were close friends on and off the set and had steamy kissing sessions. Maureen also mentions how good Barry William was at kissing! The twosome had a romantic time while filming in Hawaii.

Robert Reed was a very serious TV father. He wanted the kids to gain some acting knowledge, so he took them to Shakespeare's home. He would also take his TV kids on vacations to New York and to London, England. One Christmas, he gave them movie cameras. Another time, he gave them projectors. Robert also liked to throw parties and would play the footage the kids filmed at each of his events, literally boring everyone to death. These movies were eventually showcased in Susan Olsen's 1995 television reunion, *The Brady Home Movies*.

groovy tip!

The movie camera that Mike Lookinland received from Robert Reed sparked his interest in cinematography and led to him making his own films. Later in life, Mike has worked as a cameraman for TV and movies.

groovy tip!

After Mike Lookinland was spotted at a Grateful Dead concert, rumors started to spread that "Bobby Brady" was on tour with the group.

the end

By 1974, the kids were growing up quickly. The powers that be at Paramount decided that the only way to keep the younger audience tuning in was by bringing in a new, younger character. Enter Cousin Oliver for the last six episodes of the season.

There was serious talk that the series would come back for a sixth season. Had that happened, Robert Reed would have been replaced since his five-year contract was up. Sadly, the show was canceled. However, who would have ever predicted what would happen next with the Bradys.

In its initial run, the series was never a huge ratings' winner. When the show went into syndication in 1975, it became a huge hit. Then, with the expansion of cable TV in the late 1970s, the Bradys became available all over the world.

Being a Brady has had its pros and cons. Mike Lookinland found it easy to use his celebrity of being Bobby Brady to pick up girls. On the other hand, Susan Olsen found the dating scene difficult as she was always fighting her Cindy Brady image.

In 1992, the Brady matriarch, Robert Reed was battling colon cancer and complications from AIDS. He called his TV wife, Florence Henderson, and asked her to inform the kids about his serious condition. To this day, the kids still get emotional about his passing, and look at Reed as being their surrogate father.

The Brady Bunch has continued its subsequent success with TV movies, several spin-off series, two feature films, reunion specials, and live stage shows. Most recently, Leonard Schwartz had produced a new Brady musical with hopes of landing on Broadway. And, thanks to Paramount, fans can own the complete series on DVD, as well as newly licensed collectibles, including CDs, Beanie Babies, mugs, posters, bobble heads, dolls, lunchboxes and Christmas ornaments!

2009 marks the 40th anniversary milestone of a show that made pop phrases such as "Right on" "Far Out" and "Groovy" so cool. It was the first show that had a blended family on television and could solve any family crisis within 24 minutes.

groovy tip!

During the first several episodes of season one, Florence Henderson had to wear a wig to cover her very short hair.

Becoming Bradys: Scott & Joey become official Brady Bunch members during an autograph show.

Sherwood Schwartz, who created The Brady Bunch, which still makes viewers happy in syndication around the world.
(photo courtesy of Sherwood Schwartz)

A Brady Chat with Sherwood Schwartz

What happened after you saw the film *Yours, Mine & Ours*, which mirrors your show idea Yours & Mine?
It was my pilot film. *(laughs)* I tried to sell my show for three years and I couldn't sell it. I went to all three networks; and everybody loved it, but everybody wanted to do it their way.

For example, CBS said they liked it, but they wanted the pilot to be the sixth or seventh episode, so people could pick up the true spirit of the show. I said, "I don't understand that, because I'm telling you the true spirit of the show in the pilot." They didn't want it that way.

ABC said, "We love it, but this year we are doing two-hour shows, and we want to make the script longer." I said, "I can't make a half-hour script last two hours unless I add other elements." They didn't want other elements. I said to them, "I could write how this couple meets in the supermarket or someplace and how they have a courtship and then save this half hour you love for the last half hour, and I'll build an hour in front of it." But they said, "No we don't want that, we just want you to make it longer." I said, "I can't make it longer without making it duller."

NBC also had a problem and different way to do it. All three networks turned it down. Then the movie, *Yours, Mine & Ours*, came out, and I didn't call the network. The network called me and said, "Hey, that's what you were talking about years ago." It was about three years later and I said, "Exactly!" and then they said, "Okay, let's make a deal."

Were there any legal issues because of the feature film *Yours, Mine & Ours*?
No, as a matter of fact, [the movie's producers] sent Paramount a very legal letter saying they were suing me because my pilot was based on their

movie. I said, "It's the other way around; why don't you check the Writers Guild, when I registered this script and why don't you be happy I'm not suing you?" I never heard from them again.

How was it casting the parents for the show?
I had Florence Henderson in mind originally, and she was not available. She was on tour; so I cast Joyce Bulifant, who was very good and very funny.

Florence came back to town, and she heard I was trying to reach her. Joyce had already been cast, and we had even gone out shopping for clothes; but her agent had not solidified the deal. Then it became a big decision for Paramount and me: Which one was better? We had to decide between the two. We did the same screen test with each of them, and they both were excellent. Florence was better as a wife and Joyce was better for the comedy. It came down to last-minute discussions on major issues; but that always happens when casting. We decided to go with Florence.

The next problem: When I recast the part with Florence, I now felt I needed a funny lady in the kitchen with Mrs. Brady because there was going to be a lot of kitchen humor. The lady I had cast as Alice when Joyce was Mrs. Brady didn't need to be that funny and I had cast a plain housekeeper with a Swedish accent. She was very good, but she wasn't inherently funny. I had to have funny. That's when I went out and got Ann B. Davis, who proved to be a perfect solution.

groovy tip!

Sherwood Schwartz's 1976 new pilot show was called *Big John, Little John*, which he cast Joyce Bulifant and Robby Rist (Cousin Oliver) in the lead roles. Lloyd Schwartz was on board as producer and Hope Schwartz was credited as a dialect coach.

How did you cast Robert Reed?
I didn't find him; he found me. He had signed with Paramount to do two

pilot shows; one was based on a Robert Redford film, *Barefoot in the Park*. Mike Brady fancied himself to be another Robert Redford. They had another pilot they were doing called *Houseboat*. He also thought of himself as another Cary Grant. So he signed to do either one of those pilots, and both pilots fell through. So Paramount was stuck with a big money deal with Robert, and they put him into my show.

To be fair, Robert did the same pilot test that the other guys did and he was very good with both leading ladies, so I had no objection to him. I didn't know him at that point. I just knew he did a good scene. I foolishly didn't have him do a funny scene. I would have discovered he didn't have a sense of humor.

I used a relationship scene between husband and wife. I don't always write funny. I write a scene as it should be. In this case, it was a tender scene which he could do. Bob felt everything had to be grounded in absolute reality. That is often the enemy of comedy, and he wasn't the best judge of what could work and what couldn't work. We had nothing but fights. Once the pilot film was over, he said everything we wanted to do was an exaggeration. He said the trouble with me was that I once did *Gilligan's Island*, which was a different kind of comedy. Of course, not everything was funny in *Gilligan's Island*; most of it was a broader kind of comedy. When you write for the Brady characters; sometimes it's funny and sometimes it isn't.

In fact, in the pilot of *The Brady Bunch*, the best scene in the whole movie was with Mr. Brady and his youngest son. It was very tender and wasn't funny at all. So I was stuck with Robert Reed, and it was a constant battle for five years. After the initial run, they were going to replace him because he was so impossible. If we went into a sixth year, it was going to be without him.

How many kids did you see for the roles?

Did you know immediately when you saw each one you wanted to cast?

No, the only one I knew was Cindy [Susan Olsen], the smallest one. She was hysterical. She was serious about what she was saying, but it came out hysterical.

How was the process with casting the other Brady Kids?

They came in and all read. Then, if they passed the initial interview, they came back. I have a certain way with little kids. When I interview little kids, I put different items on the coffee table between us. There are things like a fire engine or doll. Then, during a three-minute interview, if they become unfocused on me and focus on the toys, I know they are wrong for the job. That may sound harsh, but when you're on a soundstage, there are a million things attractive to kids. If they are going to be interested in their surroundings rather than the filming, they are wrong for the show. That proved to work very well.

Here's a little-known fact: I had two sets of kids because I had not yet cast the father and the mother. There were three dark-haired girls and had three blond boys as well. So somewhere in the world roaming around they are not aware [until they read my book] that they were ever going to be a Brady.

When did you find out you were going to be picked up for the second season?

It was touch and go, and we were told at the last minute. We did not start in a blaze of glory. We were just average. By the end of the second year, we were a big hit. Although we were never in the top ten, in the five years we knocked off fifteen different competing shows. When the show went into syndication is when we went into the top ten.

Where was Tiger the dog killed?

It was outside the Paramount lot. The trainer was taking him home, and he got loose somehow, and a car ran him over. The trainer didn't want to tell us that he lost our dog, so he got another mixture dog which was very close in appearance. The trainer brought this non-actor dog and tried to do the scene, but it was hopeless because he would put him down and after a few moments the dog would get up and walk away.

In one scene the dog was just to sit and be mournful because they were going to get rid of him. He would not stay in the scene, he kept running away. So I think it was Lloyd who got the idea to nail the dog collar to the stage. So this dog was looking up with sorrowful eyes because he couldn't move his head, and it was perfect for the scene. We had a humane guy on the set at the same time so we wouldn't be accused of harming the dog in any way.

Did you keep hands-on with the show's storylines?
First of all, when I do a show, there is no one star. In any given episode, one of the characters will have a star turn, and the other actors will support him or her. It's a rotating stardom, so to speak. In that way the audience falls in love with all the characters, and you keep an audience alive that way, too.

Was focusing on the kids important?
I knew that right off the bat. That's my memory of how I planned to do it; especially when I knew I was stuck with Robert Reed, who became less and less important in the show. Very few people even remember him now; they remember the kids.

What happened with Robert Reed in the show's final episode?
He refused to act in it. Monday morning, I was shaving and I get a call from Robert Reed's agent, and he said this show has to be rewritten, because Robert won't do it the way it is. I said, ""Well, it's now Monday morning, and we are going to be shooting today." And the agent said, "He's not going to do it." While we were talking, I realized that Robert was very unimportant in that episode and so I said, "Okay, if he doesn't want to do it; he

doesn't get paid and he doesn't get residuals. He just doesn't have to do it."

Of course, I already had checked with Paramount and told them the problem. They were fed up with Robert and said, "Do what you have to do." So I figured out how to write him out of the show. By the time I got to Paramount, I already had the script rewritten in my head. It was just a question of pulling him out and giving his lines to either Florence or Ann B. That is what we did, and it was a very good show without him and he was never paid for it.

What was your favorite episode?

My favorite episode was called "Father of the Year." Marcia was writing a letter to a newspaper about why her father was a great. It was very tender but funny also. In the episode, she has to sneak out of the house to send the letter. When Mr. Brady catches her, he is furious with her and grounds her. It was very sweet and ironic: She is writing how wonderful he is, and he is punishing her. It was a very interesting episode. It's something that happened to someone in my family.

What was your favorite return show to the Bradys?

It was the *A Very Brady Christmas*. It was an emotional story about the Brady kids returning home. I was happy that the audience liked *The Brady Bunch* enough to tune in and make it the highest-rated movie of that week, that year.

What are your thoughts on A Very Brady Musical?

Very good. It has wonderful songs. It's a very simple, basic concept, and it's well done.

Is there one favorite memory of The Brady Bunch?

If I could have put Cindy's interview on a disc it would not only have been hilarious, but it would have been touching, too. My favorite moment is of her telling me the story of how things run on television. She had that lisp, which stayed with her that whole time because it was an honest lisp and that is how she spoke.

She was telling me about how she had been on *Gunsmoke* and she said [*Sherwood doing a lisp*], "My horse was frightened by a snake, Mr. Schwartz, they don't use real snakes because that would be terrible in the movies. Somebody might be bitten by a snake." She was just hysterical and that interview took two or three minutes. She was hysterical all the way. She was a very bright.

Do you still get fan mail?
I still get a lot of fan mail because it's playing in 40-50 countries today. They always want a picture of me because they don't know what I look like and I've been entertaining them for 30-40 years.

Did you keep anything from the set?
Nothing from Bradys; but I kept the carved-out figures from *Gilligan's Island* from the episode of the terrible tribal leader who had made impressions of the castaways and stuck pins in them. I have them on a shelf in my office.

You were just honored with a star on the Hollywood Walk of Fame. What did that feel like?
It was terrific. I had always had a real attachment to Hollywood Boulevard. It was where I worked when I had my first job writing for radio. It was a warm feeling so many years later at the ceremony where I was standing there with my grandchildren and my great-grandchildren. I realized that years from now, they will all be grown up and that star will still be there on the boulevard. It gave me a real remarkable feeling I never expected to have.

groovy tip!
In 2008, The Academy of Television Arts & Sciences' Hall of Fame Committee inducted Sherwood Schwartz into the **Television Academy's Hall of Fame**. Also check out Schwartz's official website at www.sherwoodschwartz.com.

Florence Henderson on stage in her 2008 cabaret at the Catalina Jazz Club in Hollywood. (photo credit: Mike Pingel)

Chapter Two:
The Brady Actors

Florence Henderson "Carol Ann Martin Tyler Brady"
Florence grew up in Indiana. She later moved to New York to attend the American Academy of Dramatic Arts. She became the "Today Girl" on NBC's *Today Show* in 1959. She was a regular singer on *The Bell Telephone Hour* and did spots on the *Dean Martin Comedy Hour*.

Florence had a strong musical theater background. She landed the lead in the national tour of *Oklahoma!* in 1952 and returned for her Broadway premiere in *Fanny* in 1954. She went on to do the national tour of *The Sound of Music* and appeared on Broadway again in *The Girl Who Came to Dinner*.

In 1968, she was cast as the mother in *The Brady Bunch*. She was living in New York, and would fly back every weekend to be with her husband, Ira Bernstein. The couple had four children, Barbara, Joseph, Robert and Elizabeth

Currently, she has her own program, *The Florence Henderson Show*, on Retirement Living TV. In 2009, she premiered a new cabaret act in Hollywood, CA. Get all her up to-date info @ http://www.flohome.com

Robert Reed "Michael Paul "Mike" Brady"
While attending Northwestern University, he married Marilyn Rosenberg, and had one child, Caroline. This marriage only lasted two years.

He later transferred and attended the Royal Academy of Dramatic Arts in London, England. Although he was not happy with the show, Reed returned for all of the different recreations of The Brady Bunch.

Reed was nominated for three Emmys in his career, *Medical Center, Rich Man, Poor Man* and *Roots*.

Reed was never out about his homosexuality. In his final days, he called his TV wife, Florence Henderson, to have her inform the Brady kids about his condition. He passed away on May 12, 1992 from colon cancer & complications of AIDS.

Barry Williams "Greg Brady"

Before becoming a Brady, Barry worked as guest star on numerous series, including Dragnet *1967, That Girl, Adam-12,* and *Mission: Impossible.*

After the Bradys Williams continued to do TV guest appearances and worked off-Broadway in the musicals *West Side Story, Oklahoma!* and *Grease.* In 1992, he wrote *Growing Up Brady,* which landed him on the *New York Times* bestseller list for three months; it was later made into a TV movie. He also released *The Return of Johnny Bravo* CD in 1999.

Williams has been married twice, Diane Martin (1990 – 1992) and Eila May Matt (1999 – 2006). He has one son, Brandon Eric Williams, born in 2003.

He has a weekly show on Sirius radio: *The Real Greg Brady's Totally '70s Pop Quiz.*

Williams official website www.thegregbradyproject.com/

Maureen McCormick "Marcia Martin Brady Logan"

At age six she won the Baby Miss San Fernando Valley contest, which opened up the acting door for her. She became an actress for kid commercials such as Kool-Aid and Barbie. She landed guest appearances on hit shows as *Honey West, Bewitched* and *My Three Sons.*

She is married to actor Michael Cummings and has one daughter, Natalie. She has been a guest correspondent for *Access Hollywood* and has been seen *in Outsider's Inn*, a reality show on CMT. Recently, Maureen released her autobiography, *Here's the Story*.

McCormick's official website: www.ttinet.com/mmfc

Eve Plumb "Jan Martin Brady Covington"

As a child actress, she worked on the hottest shows, such as *Here's Lucy, It Takes a Thief*, and *The Big Valley*.

She has married twice, first to Rick Mansfield in 1979, which ended in divorce in 1981. Her second marriage, to Ken Pace, has been going strong since 1995.

Currently, she has continued her passion for painting. She tours across America in galleries with her art. In 2008 she guest-starred as "Dora" in the daytime soap *All My Children*. Check in with Plumb and buy some art at www.eveplumb.tv

groovy tip!

In 1991, a rock band named themselves "Eve's Plum" after the actress. The band released two albums before breaking up in 1998.

Christopher Knight "Peter Brady"

At the age of seven, Knight started working as an actor in commercials for Cheerios and Tide. He moved on to guest appearances in *Mannix* and *Gunsmoke*.

Knight took some time off from the show business and went into the world of computers. He has been married three times, first to Julie Schulman (1989–1992) and then to Toni Erickson (1995–2000). In 2005, when he was filming *The Surreal Life*, he met his third wife, *America's Top Model* winner, Adrienne Curry. The twosome filmed *My Fair Brady* for VH1.

He recently competed in NBC's summer 2008 show *Celebrity Circus* and currently is the host of the game show *Trivial Pursuit: America Plays*. Visit his official webpage: www.myspace.com/christopherknight57.

Susan Olsen "Cynthia "Cindy" Martin Brady"

Olsen trained as an actress at the American Academy of Dramatic Arts. Before she was known for her lisp or those curls, she acted in an Elvis film, *The Trouble with Girls*, and did guest spots on *Gunsmoke* and *Ironside*.

She was the very first Brady to be cast. She went on to produce *Brady Bunch Home Movies* special. She has been married and divorced and has one son, Mike.

Most recently, Susan appeared on the reality series *Gimme My Reality Show* and will release a coffee-table book in 2009 about *The Brady Bunch Variety Hour*. Official site: http://www.myspace.com/officialsusanolsen.

Mike Lookinland "Robert 'Bobby' Brady"

Lookinland had done a few commercial and TV projects before being cast as the only red-headed Brady, which one might not know because they had him dye his hair for the series.

After the series ended, he worked in Oscar-nominated film *The Towering Inferno*, which starred Steve McQueen and Paul Newman. In the '80s he moved behind the camera and worked on the production side.

In 1985, on the film *Halloween 5*, he began his career as a cameraman. He even had a cameo with horror writer Stephen King on *The Stand*, which he was working on as a cameraman.

Lookinland is married to Kelly and has two boys, Joey and Scott.

Ann B. Davis "Alice Nelson"

Ann graduated from the University of Michigan with a BA in Theater. After graduating, she began her acting career performing in tent shows.

Before joining the cast of *The Brady Bunch*, Davis was a comic actress on *The Bob Cummings Show*, for which she was nominated four times and won two Emmy Awards for her work (1958 & 1959). She also had guest spots on *Bob Hope Presents the Chrysler Theatre*, *The John Forsythe Show* and *The Phyllis Diller Show*.

After *The Brady Bunch* ended, she reprised her role as Alice in all the following Brady movies and series. She continued as a working actress and even wrote the cookbook *Alice's Brady Bunch Cookbook*.

Davis is now retired from the entertainment biz, but she shows up around Hollywood for various Brady reunions.

groovy tip!

In the 2003 film *Dickie Roberts: Former Child Star*, Florence Henderson, Maureen McCormick, Barry Williams, Christopher Knight, and Mike Lookinland came together with other '70s stars to sing the final song in the film. The song was titled "Child Stars on Your Television" and is available on the movie's soundtrack. Oh yeah! Maureen McCormick sings the word "fucking" in the song … that's worth buying the CD all by itself!

28 **The Brady Bunch**

Susan Olsen, who portrayed Cindy Brady. (Photo courtesy of Susan Olsen)

A Brady Chat with Susan Olsen

Did you enjoy your pigtails (or braids)?
In the beginning, the pigtails were a hairstyle I used to request. I wanted to look like "Buffy" from *Family Affair*. After a couple of years of wearing them, I hated them. My mom always did my hair; I used to have to sleep in rubber bands and curlers to get them to look right because my hair is very straight. After a while my hair started breaking off where the rubber bands were and we had to change the hairstyle and the producer was persuaded to let me. The braids were my choice because I wanted to look like "Rhoda Penmark" from *The Bad Seed*. I went from wanting to look like Buffy to wanting to look like a serial killer.

In the final season, your hair was down … did you fight for that?
Yes, I did fight to wear my hair down, but it was almost worse because I had these stupid Mary Pickford–style curls because the song said, "The Youngest One in Curls." I remember thinking that it was odd that they wanted to be so faithful to the lyrics. Sherwood Schwartz was the same man who wrote the *Gilligan's Island* theme, which clearly stated that the passengers "set sale that day for a three-hour tour." So why did they pack?

I heard you made out in the doghouse with Michael. Is that true? Was he a good kisser?
No. Neither one of us knew how to kiss. We had no idea how to make out; we just kept hugging each other and giving closed-mouth kisses. I think we mostly held hands while we sat in the doghouse and talked about Hot Wheels.

How long did your love affair run?
Well, we rushed right into marriage (ceremony performed by Maureen,

with Eve as a witness) and that didn't even last a month. He gave me up for Eve because she was "developing."

Talking about the doghouse ... were you shaken up when Tiger was killed? Why did the doghouse stay even when Tiger was gone?
Yes, I was upset when Tiger was killed. Rupert, who played Tiger, was a really sweet dog. I had saved a treat for him on top of the Brady stairs (that led up to the catwalks). I forgot to give it to him, and he died, so it stayed up there for the duration of the show as my little tribute to him. I think the dog that immediately replaced him was only on for that one episode. The final Tiger had one blue eye. He was fired because he was new to the craft and took up production time. That was a poor decision. They should have been more patient with him because Tiger became a really fine canine actor. He starred with a young Don Johnson in *A Boy and His Dog*, and there was even a campaign to get him nominated for an Oscar. I'm not making this up! Check it: http://www.montrealmirror.com/ARCHIVES/2003/121103/film1.html

I also swear that he was a regular guest on the Cher Show, which she had right after she and Sonny split.

We kept the doghouse to cover an area where a light had fallen and melted the Astroturf grass into a plastic puddle.

What was the most favorite trick you kids played on the set?
When we had the episode with the frogs, we put one or two in Maureen McCormick's school desk. She was terrified of these frogs so we kept springing them on her.

Do you have a favorite outfit you wore?
I was definitely not into the clothes. I probably liked the Pilgrim outfit. I didn't like the Fairy Princess costume, especially because my mom made me wear it for Halloween.

The cast wore many of their outfits many, many times … why was that?
Low budget. We also got hand-me-downs , which was a good detail as that happens in real families, but it also saved money.

Is it true you were the very first Brady cast? What happened at your audition?
Yes, I was the first. The audition was three days after my seventh birthday (forty years ago *today*). I talked a mile a minute while spitting all over Sherwood Schwartz because of my lisp. He thought that was cute. My speech impediment got me the job.

What's your favorite episode? Most hated episode?
I really like the one where Greg and Peter go on a double date. Barry and Chris are really funny in it. I hated the Shirley Temple episode because I was just too old for it. It would have been cute when I was eight, but at twelve I was awkward and growing uglier by the minute and what kind of a dweeb is Cindy to be in puberty and still want to be Shirley Temple? I suppose now that makes it funnier, but at the time I felt so embarrassed singing that song (but loved Natalie Schaffer who was in the scene).

Did you have a favorite guest star?
That's tough, we loved Davy and Desi, for obvious reasons, and Imogene Coca was a trip because she was so talented yet so shy. But I think my special favorite was Hal Smith. He played Santa Claus and the Kartoon King. I loved him as Otis the Drunk on the *Andy Griffith Show*. He was a really nice man and when he played Santa he told me that he really was Santa. I said, "No, I've seen you on TV. You play that drunk guy; you're funny!" He leaned in to me and said he only acted on the side, he was really Santa. He had me going. I believed him. For the rest of my childhood I thought Santa was the town drunk of Mayberry.

Did you keep anything from the set?
No. I wasn't that clever! I did take something from the closed Paramount commissary that we used to play in. I had this wooden paddle just full of splinters that had been used to stir soup. I have a lot of memorabilia, but nothing really from the set. We would definitely have gotten in trouble if we had taken anything.

Any crazy fan stories?
When I was seven, I got some weird letters from men who wanted my underwear. That was pretty sick.

Your favorite "vacation" episode.
Hawaii! While Cincinnati was quite a thrill, the beaches on Oahu are prettier.

How was it working with Robert and Florence? As a kid, what did you learn from them?
Bob taught me how to treat kids with respect and they will give back respect (that almost works with my son). Bob treated us as fellow actors; he never talked down to us. I try to never talk down to kids, especially if I'm working with them. There is no need to; children are no less intelligent than adults, they are just less experienced. Florence took on a very motherly role and I saw her as a mother with her real-life kids who we grew up with. She is still very much a mother figure to me. Now let's not forget Ann B! She was not comfortable with kids at first, but she was such a fun person and she grew to love us and we loved her. She taught us needle crafts and how to be a prepared professional. My birthday was a few days ago and one of the best treats was a phone message from Ann B. singing "Happy Birthday."

How was Robert Reed as a director?
Wonderful. He listened to us. He wanted to try different things and he wanted to let us grow. He was much happier on the set when he was directing.

What was your favorite Brady recreation series?
The Variety Hour, because it's so horrible.

If I can ask – Why didn't you return for A Very Brady Christmas?
Basically, it was finances. The network only had to deliver five out of six of us kids. One of us was expendable. I had a honeymoon planned and they were offering me a fraction of what they were paying Maureen and Eve. It seemed ridiculous to cancel my trip to the Reggae Sunsplash in Jamaica to be insulted. I wasn't too keen on the role, either: A building falls on Dad and Cindy leads the family in a sing-along. I was going to have a hard time with that (Jennifer Runyan pulled it off well). I was old enough … and young enough that it felt kind of good to be a rebel and not come back for one reunion. I think Maureen got jealous of Eve and I both having our renegade Brady moments (Eve wisely avoided the *Variety Hour*), so she didn't do the next project: *The Bradys*.

How was it working with the Schwartz family?
They were ideal. They really cared about keeping the set a healthy one. Sherwood even tried to see to it that most of the people working on the set were family people so there would be a good atmosphere for us kids. Sherwood was always available and if we went to visit him in his office, he would never stay behind his desk. He would come out and sit on the couch to talk. He wanted to give us respect. (In hindsight, I might have preferred that he gave us more money ☺.) His son, Lloyd, started out as a dialogue coach on the show. His brother was a writer and I used to go to his house because I was friends with his niece. I know that my childhood work experience was made happier by several Schwartzes.

What are your future/current projects?
We have the fabulous *Variety Hour* book that I'm working on. *The Brady*

Bunch Variety Hour will finally get the recognition it deserves: a coffee-table book revealing all of its horrific splendor. How America's number one most beloved family ended up making what *TV Guide* voted "the fourth worst show in TV history." It's like the day that television ate the brown acid. It's just a madly colorful bad trip, but put together by some very creative and well-meaning people. The show has been deliberately kept in the Brady closet for years (that door at the top of the stairs), but now it's coming out. You've been warned.

Why do think the gay community gravitates to the show?
Well, Bob was in that closet at the top of the stairs, too, but that's an obvious reason. I think a lot of gay children are very sensitive and in knowing that they are different, they are forced to look at life more deeply. This can add a lot of stress to a childhood. *The Brady Bunch* has always served as a place to have a happy and supportive childhood even if you don't have that in your real life.

Mike and Carol won't get mad if you come out. They didn't get mad at Peter when he put on a dress and went out selling Sunshine Girl cookies. They embraced Sgt. Emma ...well, until she made them exercise.

What was your highlight with being a Brady?
Having another family. They are still my other family. My son has a Grandma Flo and extra aunts and uncles. We don't see each other that much, but we also don't feel pressured into *having* to see each other. It's really quite nice.

groovy tip!

Susan Olsen is a devoted animal lover! She donates her time and is now on the Board of Directors of the Precious Paws organization. Precious Paws provides homes, food and money for homeless animals. Check out their website at www.Preciouspaws.org.

Funny Lady, Ann B. Davis who played the loveable Alice.

A Brady Chat with Ann B. Davis

How did you become cast in the show?
I was cast in the role because Sherwood Schwartz came to think I would be good in that part. He had not met me personally yet, but I was doing nightclub work in Seattle and he had me fly down to meet him. He overpaid me, which allowed me to buy my way out of my nightclub work, and I flew back down to LA to shoot the pilot. Then I had to fly back to Seattle to drive my car back down.

Were there any hesitations about taking the role?
Oh, my goodness, no. I'm a working actor that likes to work!

Did you feel the show was something special while filming the pilot? That it would be around for so many years?
No, I don't think anybody ever thinks like that. I don't think you can or you'll kill it. I do remember there was a discussion on the set of the pilot by Sherwood Schwartz, should it be call *The Brady Bunch* or *The Brady Brood*? *Brady Brood* was the title at first. My first reaction was that *Bunch* was a much better word than *Brood*. That may not be why he chose it, but that's the way it turned out.

Why do you think people are drawn to The Brady Bunch even today?
I think children are optimistic and parents would like their children to grow up with values. It was a good show about nice people doing nice things for each other and it had values. It sounds pretty corny, but that's what we don't find on TV these days.

Do you think it was Alice's cooking which kept the family together? And is it true you can't cook?
(*Laughing*) No, it was the writers, Sherwood Schwartz and all the people who worked around me, and I don't cook. I did put out a *Brady Bunch* cookbook, but someone else did the recipes and I wrote the commentary. I do boil water.

Do you have a favorite episode?
I don't imagine that I have one. The most fun episode was the time I got dunked into the carnival water booth. I thought that was fun and I insisted that Sherwood Schwartz come down from his office and watch me do it. Because it was going to destroy me from working the rest of the day and that was for sure. He came down.

Was there any crazy kid moments you can recall?
All the moments with kids were crazy. I know on the pilot, the light screen fell on Susan Olsen. She was six years old and gave her a black-eye. She was a brave little girl as she sat there very quietly as our make-up man with hands the size of hams painted out the black-eye so she could go on filming.

Anything you wanted to do with your character Alice you didn't do?
No, I don't think so. What I did was take my own life and integrate it so I would have some subtext going for me. Like, I could make a loud whistle with just using my teeth. So that ended up in a lot of the shows. I was doing some skiing so that was written into a skiing show. I did everything under the sun on the show. It was a ball.

How was it meeting Henry Kissinger?
One day, he and his son came to the set. He was being shown around and I took the kid back to see the little classroom that the kids were taught in. The room was filled in with pictures fans had sent in and were pasted on the wall. As we were in the room, suddenly I had a large person bursting through the door looking for the son, because they had not seen him leave. Now that was exciting.

How was it working with Allan Melvin as "Sam"?
He was fine. For one thing, he was very tall and he made me feel very small. He was such a physical actor and a very pleasant guy. He only did one show a year so I worked with him about five times.

And working with Robert and Florence?
Florence is a doll and solid gold. Robert was a serious, classically-trained actor. He was never that happy on the show, so sometimes it was difficult. If you are professional you learn how to cope with that. I didn't have much to do with Bob but professionally. He and I worked well together.

How was it stepping out of Alice and into "Sergeant Emma"?
That was great fun. That type of stuff is wonderful; we get to do technique things as you're standing on both side of the line acting to yourself. Get to dress up and wear wigs.

Did you keep anything from the set?
My chair. I needle pointed a backing for it with my name and stick figures representing the folks.

Any thoughts about your blue housekeeper outfit you wore?
Just that it was wonderful not to have to worry about what you're going to be wearing. They had me come in and try a whole flock of outfits and I picked the one I was most comfortable in and I wore it for five years. Occasionally, I would have to wear something else, but it was mostly very handy not having to have costume changes.

What was it like doing the re-do series of the Bradys?
We did about five or six different shows and by that time I was living in a Christian community so I would fly in and work a few days then fly back. It was fun to make contact with the cast after they became adults. It was always very hard to get down to work because we were all so busy catching up on our news.

How was it to work on *The Bob Cumming Show*?
That was fun. I had done stage work before that, but I had never done film work. So I was very careful to listen to everybody. Everybody was very helpful that I could learn film techniques while we were shooting. If I made a mistake, being stage trained, I would keep on talking and go around it. As the scene progressed, Bob would make a mistake so I didn't have to be embarrassed about making any mistakes. Then we would go back and reshoot and I would do it right the second time. Took me a while to catch on; Bob was quite gracious about that.

How was it winning two Emmys?
Oh my dear, if you like fainting in public, try that! I didn't, but I certainly felt like it.

You have your own star on the Hollywood Walk of Fame?
Yes, I do, as a matter of fact.

Do you walk by it when you come into town?
I haven't been there in years, but my friends went by it the other day and said, "It's still there."

Is there something your fans ask all the time when they meet you?
"Why do you look familiar?" That happened to me today!

What will you remember most about *The Brady Bunch*?
The fact that it has lasted so long and it was a decent show and that I had a good part on it. If I had become known as "Alice the Axe Murderer," I would have become very unhappy. Being known for all these years as Alice from *The Brady Bunch* has been wonderful.

What are you up to now?
Retired. I live very pleasantly in a Christian community with people I have known for 30 years.

Lloyd J. Schwartz with his dad. (photo courtesy of Lloyd J. Schwartz)

Chapter Three:

A Brady Chat With Lloyd J. Schwartz

How did the *Brady Bunch* come to be?
The original series came about in a newspaper article my dad read. It was a little filler article which said that all the families at that point in the middle-1960s brought children from other first marriages.

Dad was so sure that other people would see that article and that all writers would come up with this idea that he immediately raced to The Writers Guild to register it. Then he couldn't sell it to any of the networks. It wasn't until the movie *Yours, Mine & Ours* came out. Then the networks remembered Dad's idea and said, "'Didn't Sherwood Schwartz come in with an idea like this?" Then there was a lot of network interest until ABC finally put it on the air.

What was a typical film week like on *The Brady Bunch*?
The Brady Bunch was a one-camera show as opposed to a three-camera show; so there weren't rehearsals and then shooting on one night. The series usually took four days to film one episode. Everyone has a memory

of a bunch of kids running around. That didn't happen more than once an episode because child labor laws only gave us limited time with each child on any given day. We did scenes with different kids and staggered the schedule so we could accomplish a day's work. Robert Reed's and Florence Henderson's scenes were usually filmed after the kids had gone home for the day.

Did you have to work with child labor laws then?

Certainly. And we were very strict with it. I was associate producer for most of the show and producing toward the end and worked very closely with the welfare worker and teacher, Frances Whitfield. We never went over the time we were allowed. The kids could not work past 6:30 p.m. and so we would have some come in a little early and some a little late and it was very well broken down.

How was it working with your whole own family?

At that point, I didn't really. Out of my family it was only Dad and I on a daily basis. Sometimes, my sister acted in a few episodes, but she was only there on those days. So it was not a family affair during the original series. A couple of my uncles were writers and wrote some episodes, but they weren't on the set. I confess, it was difficult for me working with my father because there is always a cry of nepotism. As long as I did my job, people respected me for who I was ... and not just the boss's son. It did call for a sublimation of my own ego.

Dad and I had an arrangement: When I was working with him, I would always be doing my own projects as well. I made a movie and wrote plays. As far as I know, Sherwood and Lloyd Schwartz were the only father/son producing team in the business, and I think our arrangement made it possible.

It went so far as I never let my parents know where I was living. That may sound peculiar, but I had a reason ... which my parents respected. I was at work all day with my dad on a 12-hour day and on the weekend they were my parents so I would see them then. I just needed a place where they weren't. I have always had a wonderful relationship with my parents ... which I am blessed to say continues to this day.

How was it working with your sister in the new musical?
Hope and I have written several things together. I added her to the writing staff of *The Brady Brides*, and we wrote *Brady Bunch in the White House* together. She and I share ... unfortunately or fortunately ... the same sense of humor. She is the only person with whom I can actually sit in the room and write. We just laugh all the time. When I write with Dad, we get together to work out the outline. Then I write the first draft, and writes the second draft. My sister and I can actually sit there together, and it's not like work. It's just fun until we get to "the end," and then we're a little sorry it's over.

As far as writing *A Very Brady Musical*, Hope has more influence over the musical aspects since she is a lot more musical than I am. We would argue about some of the style ... particularly the level of satire of other musicals, but I think that our creative differences led to a more successful piece of work.

What was behind the Robert Reed fights?
It wasn't us. It was him. But in arguments or fights, isn't that what everyone says? Well, first of all, it had nothing to do with his sexual orientation. We knew right from the beginning he was gay and it made no difference. The fact that he was a bastard ... that made a difference.

I don't want to get Freudian about all this ... and I didn't figure it out until after he died ... but Bob had some real problems ... excuse my amateur psychology. It's pretty deep, really. When I went to lunch with Florence, she told me that when Bob was dying, he called and asked her to tell the kids.

A light bulb went off, and his behavior finally made sense. At one level, he really believed he was the head of the Brady family. Looking back, that was the reason for our fights. Because if he was the head of this imaginary family; we were in his way, and it became his mission to get rid of us. If ... in his own head ... he was running the family. It was pretty twisted, but I think that was his reality.

Besides, Bob Reed was an unhappy man. He didn't have a family of his own and at the same time, this guy, Mike Brady, was loved and respected by his family. He was just angry most of the time. I don't ever remember him really having a friend. Also, Bob saw himself as a leading man in feature films, and that didn't pan out after he had the lead opposite Julie Andrews in the unsuccessful *Star!* (1968). So, suddenly, he was back in TV and saddled with six kids. That said, he dearly loved the Brady kids as individuals. He even took them on a vacation and bought them presents and everything. Personally, I think he was just trying to buy their affection in his struggle to take the show away from us. The kids didn't object to being doted on ... who would?

Our fights with him never happened in front of the kids. He was smart enough not to let that happen. Even Barry, who wrote a book, never knew how mean-spirited Bob was when they left for the day. Later, Barry and I would talk and something would come up about things that happened on the set, and he would say with some authority, "Well, this is what happened." I would say, "Barry, you weren't there." Barry had gotten his "facts" from other unreliable sources. And he'd say, '"But, it's in my book." "Barry, just because it's in your book, doesn't mean it happened."

Robert Reed's sexual orientation didn't really affect the show ... though you seldom see any physical affection between the parents. It's a pretty sterile environment, but that was reflective of the times. Florence is much more physical than Robert. He was a bit stiffer. I don't know ... maybe it worked for the character.

I will say this: We did restrict what we filmed in terms of Bob because he wasn't the most athletic man, and he sometimes came out a little flamboyant. Think back about the episodes, and you never saw him playing ball with the kids. He wouldn't have come out like the he-man guy he wanted to portray.

Reed did come back for all the future Brady _projects._
I give him credit for that. When we were getting ready to do the reunion, he was in a play in New York and I believe he bought himself out of some performances. He was reported to have said, "No one is going to give those girls away except for me." Or maybe it was because he actually saw himself as their father.

Here is some interesting news: When the show was canceled after five years, we were negotiating another season ... a season he wasn't going to be in. He was just too much of a pain. We weren't sure whether or not his character was gong to die or we would pull a *Bewitched* and just replace him. Because this show ended before we made the decision, he remained with the series the whole time ... and ... looking back ... I think that was good thing.

Did the kids have any crazy fans?
Sure. We intercepted most of the fan mail at that point because there were some weird letters. Some came from prisoners sending pictures of themselves and making some pretty odd requests.

Were there any problems with the network with the series?
None. In fact, one time we were invited to the annual censorship meeting. Before they even began to lay out what you could and could not say, they said, "Anybody from *The Brady Bunch* can go."

The only note we ever got was an episode where Mike Brady gives some advice to Marcia, who was nervous about taking her driver's test. He advises her that "If you look at people and think about them in their underwear you won't get nervous." Then we would do a shot from her point of view of the driving test administrator, and he'd be in his underwear. The network note: "When filming this, make sure he's wearing boxers." That was the only censorship note in all those years.

Dad couldn't get the word "bunch" through for the title since, at the time he was trying to sell the show, the word "bunch" had *Wild Bunch* connotations. Finally, they let him have the title *Brady Bunch* and now ... because of *The Brady Bunch*, the word "bunch" has a warm and fuzzy connotation.

Favorite guest star on the show?
Vincent Price. What a charming man. If you ever talk with anybody who ever worked with him, they'll tell you he was the most professional man in the business. He came on the set really early in the morning and he knew his lines and everyone else's. He said to me, "You want to know why I'm here so early?" and I said, "Why?" He said, "There's no place else I rather be." What a pleasure.

Do you have a favorite episode?
My favorite is the Jesse James episode. There is a dream sequence where Mike [Bobby Brady] sees his family gunned down in a dream sequence by Jesse James. It was done in a grandiose comedic fashion by a guy shouting "Bang, bang, bang." It was tricky, but I wanted Mike Lookinland to react as if his family were really being shot and dying and not in the funny way we were filming. We shot it with no rehearsal since I filled Mike's head with some pretty terrible images. If you have a chance to watch the episode, you see a terrified look on his face. I like it because I'm very anti-gun, and it sure makes a point. I debriefed him after the sequence to calm him down.

We were seldom controversial or political, but there were a few times when we took a position. We did the first anti-smoking show. We did a woman's lib show. A lot of times, we would put in different ethnicities (which was not being done) as the kids' friends. Not the most groundbreaking things, but we tried to do our part along the way.

Did some of the Brady storylines come from the kids' lives?
Not from the kids, but several came from our home life. When I worked with the kids, we did change some dialogue to make it fit them better. If something wasn't the way they would say it, I had the right to change anything.

The episode when Marcia was accused of drawing a picture, that actually happened to my dad. ("The Slumber Caper," #28)

Did you save anything from the Brady *set?*
No. If I knew that people would pay a lot for Brady memorabilia I would have taken a lot, sold it, and made a lot of money.

Did the Bradys ever win an award?
At that time, the only award *The Brady Bunch* won was a Patsy Award for the goat ("Getting Greg's Goat," #101). (The Patsy Award was given by the American Humane Association to honor animal performers. Pasty stands for Picture Animal Top Star of the Year.) Since then, we won a TV Land Pop Culture Award, and Dad has gotten a star on Hollywood Boulevard and in December will enter the TV Academy Hall of Fame.

We did win an Emmy nomination for the 35th reunion show. We lost ... and properly so ... to *The Salute to the 9/11 Victims*. My acceptance speech was going to be: "You know, when we did the original series; we never won any kind of award and now we're nominated for this reunion show. I think we should have skipped the series and gone right to the reunion." That was my speech. It never was heard.

Was it hard to find a cast for the movie?
I was not super involved. We did cast Christine Taylor [Marcia Brady]. I will tell you that there were major battles in making the movie and we had to go toe-to-toe with the studio. Our view was to do an affectionate satire, and they wanted to do a biting, slashing satire. They were adamant. Finally, we had to threaten that we would go on talk shows to tell people not to

see the movie if they made that picture. They gave in, and the movies were quite successful.

How did the *Brady Musical* come about?
We have a *Gilligan's Musical*, which is starting a national tour in January 2009 and has had sixty productions. Because it was so successful, we were asked to license the *Brady Bunch Musical*. The only problem: There wasn't one. So my sister and I said, "Why don't we just do it?" CBS/Paramount had to sign off first because they have the rights. They agreed. I had been working at Theatre West, a top theatre company in the Valley, for twenty-five years so I knew the actors. I thought about all the roles and realized I had a great cast within the company. I'm proud that every single actor in *A Very Brady Musical* is a member of Theatre West. If I looked anywhere in the world, I won't find anybody better for any of the roles.

Will *A Very Brady Musical* be touring soon?
It's all up in the air right now. There are talks of doing a movie based on the show and Broadway is interested. I'm keeping my fingers crossed.

What was your favorite recreation of the Bradys?
I love *The Brady Brides*. That was the first time I was able to strut my stuff independently. At the exact same time, Dad and I were doing *Harper Valley P.T.A.* We divided up primary responsibilities. Dad ran *Harper* and I did *Brady*.

In casting the two husbands, the actual actors who got the parts were close friends of mine even before the show started. I guess I wrote it with them in mind since the network and studio picked them without any influence from me.

We were really starting to hit our stride ... and doing well in the ratings ... when we were canceled. Grant Tinker [then Chairman of NBC] said it just wasn't his kind of show. Oh, well.

When *A Very Brady Christmas* was telecast a few years later, it was the highest-rated TV movie of the year. In deference to Grant Tinker, I guess *Brady* was still America's kind of show.

Did you ever think the Bradys would become pop culture?
No. We didn't do anything to make that happen. Just the opposite. Dad said there would be no catch phrases. "Marcia, Marcia, Marcia" was only said in one episode and "Pork chops and applesauce" was only said in one episode. It was a surprise to us that the show has done so well since its original run.

Did you have any idea when the kids were dating?
Chris and Eve didn't date until they left the show. Barry and Maureen, yes! They were hot for each other, and it was my job to keep them off of one another. So I would always say to Barry, "Look, this not something you want to be involved in." Then when Maureen developed later, Barry got more and more interested. Fortunately, it wasn't until the last year when there was really a mutual spark. I tried everything. I even said to Barry, "She has great-looking friends. Just use her to get to her friends."

We only had trouble when we went to Hawaii. It was my mistake because I met some girl there and I asked her to go for a walk on the beach. So everybody paired up and walked and it was too romantic and I was really stupid.

That whole Barry/Florence thing, that was not real at all. Even in Barry's book it really came down to he wanted her to see this singer, they went to see the singer and she kissed him on the cheek goodnight and that was it. That was their mad affair.

Were the kids terrors on the Paramount lot?
Yes ... but in a fun, kid way. And I'm proud that I inspired that. When word got to the studio president that the Brady kids were running around, I was summoned to his office. He told me to stop them ... that they were

property. That got my 1960s challenge authority back up. I told him, "You know, they're kids and that's what they should be doing. I don't want them to break their arms, but they need the chance. What you see on the screen is because they are kids acting like kids, so if you want to do something different with them, then you're going to have to fire me." Then I went back and Dad asked me why I was in the studio president's office. I told him that and he said, "I would have never done that."

Any future projects with the original stars?
I would doubt it. The kids are in their fifties, and it would have to be a pretty unusual project to get them all together for a movie of some kind. They could do specials and things, but who knows? There is a possibility of a reality show with *A Very Brady Musical*. They would talk about maybe putting this Broadway show together and they would be in it and would help with the casting.

Do you ever get tired of Brady, Brady, Brady?
I get tired when others call to suggest other Brady projects to me. I don't particularly want to do Brady projects, but I sure don't want anyone else to do them. It's my legacy to protect the integrity of it all.

What is the secret of the longevity of Bradys?
There are a couple of things. Believe it or not, one of them is that it was the first family show in color. Also, it was a family show that dignified the kids' problems as being important and how the parents get involved in them. So many shows on the air have the father or mother as idiots, but we really approached it with the point of view of the kids. We thought that was important. I also think that the age range of the kids gave a lot of people someone with whom to identify. And there was no freak kid, so there wasn't an "Urkel" or an "Alex Keaton" character who would become a fad and then rise and fall meteorically. All of the kids were pretty much

recognizable. In fact, none of the characters of the kids were defined when we started the show. We basically made them who they were and started writing for them.

Are you and your father planning on publishing a book?
Yes, it's called *BRADY, BRADY, BRADY*. It covers the whole history of Brady. Dad wrote up through the pilot and I wrote from then on. It's interesting since there are two distinct styles. It has a lot of insights and a perspective that no one else has.

Maureen McCormick with her book, Here's the Story: *Surviving Marcia Brady and Finding My True Voice* (photo by Mike Pingel)

Brady Books

Most of the Brady kids have taken time to share their feelings and their experiences with their fans inside pages of books.

Barry Williams: *Growing Up Brady* (1992 & 2000)

Barry Williams took his memories of the series and wrote the very successful book, *Growing Up Brady*. The book allows fans to experience Williams' world as Greg Brady, which includes his crushes on Maureen McCormick and Florence Henderson. He also shows how life on the *Brady* set was with the constant fights between Sherwood Schwartz and Robert Reed and the budding love affairs between his co-stars.

The book was re-released in 2000 in a "Special Edition" and was produced into a TV film of the same title. Adam Brody (*The O.C.*) played Barry, Kaley Cuoco (*The Big Bang Theory*) played Maureen and Mike Lookinland's son Scott played Bobby.

Maureen McCormick: *Here's the Story: Surviving Marcia Brady and Finding My True Voice* (2008)

HarperEntertainment released Maureen's autobiography. McCormick, who made combing your hair 100 times a must, will chatted about the highs and the lows of her forty-plus-year career, and the dark side of finding success in Hollywood at a young age.

From the book's press release, McCormick says about her new book, "I've learned that overcoming my demons and weathering the tumultuous storms of my life is a process. I have come to terms with the fact that though I may never completely win this battle, I will never lose. I have arrived, for the moment at least, in a solid and secure place, which is allowing me to visit my past without fear. Writing this book has been such a cathartic experience. I hope it will not only shed light on who I am and how I got here, but more importantly, remind the readers that there truly is a light at the end of any tunnel."

Susan Olsen, Ted Nichelson & Lisa Sutton: *Love to Love You Bradys* (2009)

Here's the story of *The Brady Bunch* no one has dared to tell, brought to you by the one and only Cindy Brady herself, Susan Olsen.

Love to Love You Bradys: The Bizarre Story of the Brady Bunch Variety Hour is an in-depth retrospective of the most disastrous offering in television history. Olsen's coffee-table book will delve into the how and why this spin-off was conceived and produced, forever scarring the legacy of *The Brady Bunch*.

The book features 200 color photographs and detailed text comprised from over 90 extensive interviews, including *Brady Bunch* cast members, producers, behind-the-scenes crew, creator Sherwood Schwartz, Sid and Marty Krofft, and the infamous "Fake Jan" Geri Reischl. Olsen will celebrate the 40th anniversary of the Bradys with the release of the book in 2009 through ECW Press. Official website: www.lovetoloveyoubradys.com

Ann B. Davis: *Alice's Brady Bunch Cookbook*

Ann B. Davis released this cookbook, which was a funny thing since the cast mentions Davis could not cook! The foreword for the book was written by Sherwood Schwartz.

groovy tip!

Picture this: Liberace and the Brady Bunch Kids doing the limbo on *The Mike Douglas Show*. It really happened way back on June 13, 1973 (search for it on YouTube). Now how 'happy' is that!

Geri Reischl 1970s headshot the "Fake Jan" (courtesy from Geri Reischl)

Chapter Four:
Brady's reincarnated

A Brady chat with Geri Reischl

How does it feel being a Brady?
It feels great being a Brady. I mean what's *not* to like about being a Brady? You mention *The Brady Bunch* and everybody knows what you're talking about.

How did you get the part of Jan?
My agent called saying that I would be going out on an audition for the character of Jan Brady from the *Brady Bunch*. She told me a 'new' Jan was being cast for a variety show they were going to be doing. During the interviews I would have to sing, dance, read from a script and cry. I went on a few interviews before I finally got the part. At least 3,500 girls from all over auditioned for the part.

How was the cast?
I was welcomed with open arms. They were all very nice to me. The first day I met them we went right to work learning lines, dance steps and songs. I guess I fit in just fine.

One of the most wonderful things that was said to me while I was doing *The Brady Bunch Hour* came from Mr. Reed. He took me aside and told me, "Geri, it's like you have always been a part of this family. I am glad to have you with us." That comment made my day.

Were you a fan of *The Brady Bunch*?
To be honest, I never really watched the show. I was working on TV during that time period. I did see bits and pieces of the show and I really liked it, but I was so busy doing other things that I really didn't watch that much TV.

Did you have a favorite episode?
I really liked the second episode. Our guest-stars were Tina Turner and Milton Berle. I got to wear a big yellow chicken suit and I got to hit Chris Knight with Mr. Berle's huge powder puff. I almost knocked Chris on his butt. The powder went everywhere, looking like a huge puff of smoke. Tina Turner is fabulous! I loved her performance on the show. One classy lady.

Did you come from a musical background?
I haven't a clue. I was adopted so who knows where my musical talents came from. All I know is that I love to perform. The bigger the audience the better.

How was it working with your old schoolmates, Susan and Mike?
It was great fun working with Susan and Mike. Susan and I became really good friends and our moms did, too, because they would sit together everyday while we would be working. I really liked Mike, too. He was a really nice guy, super funny and had a great sense of humor. We had a lot of fun hanging out together and riding around in his new car. Susan would spend the night at my house, we rode in parades together and our families would go out to dinner sometimes. Susan and I still hang out and do things together.

What was most fun being the "Jan"?
It was definitely going to work everyday, working with such wonderful people and being able to do what I loved doing the most and that was singing and dancing. I have to say that I loved the recognition, especially from the fans. I was always making new friends everywhere I went. That was awesome.

What do you think about the title "Fake Jan"?
I love that title. I want to have my own identity because I don't want anyone ever thinking that I think I'm the real Jan Brady because I'm not. I did play Jan Brady, but I was not the original Jan. Fake Jan is really groovy!

"Fake Jan" has taken a life of its own, with a band name, songs, website. What are you feeling about the fun "Fake Jan" reflection?
It puts a big smile on my face. I am proud to be called "Fake Jan" and people seem to like it, too. It makes them chuckle when they hear it and then the questions start coming. Now is that cool or what having a band named after you? Totally awesome! I guess "Fake Jan" is catchy. I like having that for a nickname. Oh yes, the website is http://www.fakejan.com. MySpace is http://www.myspace.com/fakejan. I guess "Fake Jan" is easy to remember.

What was a typical day filming *The Brady Bunch Hour*?
A typical day would have been getting to the studio early in the morning and either going straight to school or hair and make-up. It would all depend on if we were going to be in one of the first scenes for the day. During breaks we would sometimes hang out with Donny and Marie Osmond. They filmed their show on the soundstage next to ours. At lunch time Donny and I would toss around a football in the parking lot after Susan Olsen and I got back from having lunch at Denny's. Sometimes we'd eat something from the lunch wagon. We would have lots of costume changes because we had so many musical numbers to film. So much went on every

single day. We would shoot a scene and then go back to school, or learn new dance steps and new lyrics.

Did you ever think you were creating an "iconic" TV character?
I had absolutely no idea I was creating anything. I was doing what I loved to do so that thought never came across my mind ... ever. People ask me, "What's it like being a 'Pop Culture Icon?'" I've never thought of myself as one, so I really can't say what it feels like. I just know it was great being a Brady. I was the very first person to ever replace an original Brady character and not just for a one-time appearance, but I played the character Jan Brady for one whole season. Simply amazing.

Did the production have you do anything to make you more like the original Jan?
At first they had my character being whiny and complaining. The middle child syndrome thing. They dropped that right away. Thank goodness. One thing they had me do to look more like the other Jan Brady was to hide my bangs. Everyday they would put a ton of hairspray on my bangs so they would stay hidden and sometimes they would use bobby-pins and pin them back.

Who was your favorite guest star?
I got to choose the guest-star for my episode. I chose Lynn Anderson because I loved her music. I was really into country music and I loved singing country songs. I had always looked up to Ms. Anderson because of her amazing voice and true talent. I was in awe the whole time she was on the set. She was extremely nice.

Any funny stories from the set?
There are a lot of funny stories from the show, but one is standing out in my mind for the moment. It goes back to the chicken suit I wore. We were doing a musical number which required us to stand on high pedestals. The

chicken suit I wore had some big wings on it and I had to flap them up and down really fast during the number we were doing. I guess I flapped them so fast that I actually took flight. I'm not kidding you. I flew and fell down onto the stage and almost into the pool we used on the show. Our director yelled "CUT." Robert Reed got down fast from his pedestal and came over to see if I was okay. I told him I was fine and then everyone started laughing because they saw me flying off my pedestal. I am so glad that I didn't land in the pool because I would have sunk.

What did you think of the "Lisa" on *The Simpson Smile-Time Variety Hour*?
I loved the spoof on *The Simpsons* with Lisa. It was cool that I could be a part of the *Simpsons' Smile-Time Variety Hour*. She was wearing my outfit. It didn't look too bad on her either.

What is your favorite memory of *The Brady Bunch Hour*?
My favorite memory would be working with the most incredible people ever: Robert Reed, Florence Henderson, Barry Williams, Maureen McCormick, Chris Knight, Mike Lookinland, Susan Olsen, Ann B. Davis and Rip Taylor. It doesn't get any better than that. If I had to be associated with any TV series I can truly say that I am so proud and honored to have been a part of *The Brady Bunch*.

Were you really up for the lead in *The Exorcist*?
I was one of the three finalists for the part of Regan. Director William Friedkin really wanted me for the part. He tried to talk my mom into letting me play the part of Regan, but she said no because she had read the book and found out that during some of the scenes I would be in I would have to be "hypnotized" in order to do what they wanted.

groovy tip!

In 2005 a mobile video game called *Brady Bunch Kung Fu* by Mobliss was introduced which had the Bradys going head-to-head with each other in combat. Greg uses his dancing moves as Cindy uses her doll and Alice uses her mop to kick some ass. Sprint mobile users can still download this game for free.

The Second Brady's

The series lived on in numerous spin-offs and movies throughout the years. Here are short breakdowns of each re-carnation of the series:

The Brady Kids – 1972 – TV cartoon series

The Brady Kids hit the adventure trail as cartoon characters of themselves. They are helped in their adventures by Marlin the magic bird, Mop Top the dog and two pandas, Ping & Pong.

Most notable episode is "It's All Greek to Me" where the Brady Kids meet Wonder Woman. This was the first-ever appearance of Wonder Woman on television.

Twenty-Two episodes were produced and were included in a one-hour show shown on Saturday mornings as part of *The ABC Saturday Superstar Movie*.

The Brady Kids cartoon did create a spin-off cartoon titled *Mission: Magic!* The cartoon starred the voice of singer/actor Rick Springfield (*General Hospital*).

The Brady Bunch Hour - 1977 – TV series (Nine episodes)

The variety hour included nine jammed-packed episodes. For this series Eve Plumb did not return and was replaced by Geri Reischl as Jan. Geri became a true asset to the variety hour with her strong background in singing.

The Brady Bunch Hour hosted many house guests, including Farrah Fawcett-Majors (*Charlie's Angels*), Lee Majors (*Six Million Dollar Man*), Rip

Taylor, Vincent Price, Charo, Rich Little, Red Foxx, Tony Randall (*The Odd Couple*).

Brady Note:

The Brady Kids preformed live on *The World of Sid & Marty Krofft* at the Hollywood Bowl on July 29, 1973. Fellow Bradys Robert Reed and Ann B. Davis were in the audience.

The Brady Girls Get Married – 1981 – TV movie

Marcia and Jan are getting married and the girls decide they should marry in the family's backyard. The original cast reprises their roles for this film. This was the first time since the series that the cast was all together on screen.

The Brady Brides – 1981 – TV series

Marcia and Jan are all grown up, fall in love and have married. The sisters find the perfect house and convince their husbands it would be a great idea to move in together.

Alice Nelson Franklin, the Bradys' housekeeper (Ann B. Davis), lives close by and comes around often to help out the girls! Marcia marries Wally Logan (Jerry Houser), a toymaker, and Jan marries Phillip Covington III (Ron Kuhlman), a professor.

Sherwood & Lloyd J. Schwartz both executive produced the show and Frank DeVol did the music again. The series only ran for ten episodes, including the pilot film, which was chopped up into the first three episodes.

Season 1

The Brady Girls Get Married, pt. 1	February 6, 1981
The Brady Girls Get Married pt. 2	February 13, 1981
The Brady Girls Get Married pt. 3	February 20, 1981
Living Together	March 6, 1981

Gorilla of My Dreams	March 13, 1981
The Newlywed Game	March 20, 1981
The Mom Who Came to Dinner	March 27, 1981
The Siege	April 3, 1981
Cool Hand Phil	April 10, 1981
A Pretty Boy Is Like a Melody	April 17, 1981

A Very Brady Christmas – 1998 - TV Movie

Carol and Mike take their vacation money and fly the entire family home for the holidays. As Brady kids gather at home for the holidays, they start to work out their personal problems. Mike Brady finds there's structural damage to one of his current building projects and goes to investigate, but becomes trapped under the fallen building.

The entire original cast returns, except Susan Olsen. Actress Jennifer Runyon (*Charles In Charge*) plays the role of Cindy. The film was written and produced by Sherwood & Lloyd J. Schwartz and was directed by Peter Baldwin, who also directed *The Brady Brides* and many of the original shows.

A Brady Chat with Zach Bostrom (Kevin Brady) "A Very Brady Christmas"

Had you seen The Brady Bunch **prior to doing the film?**
Yes, I totally used to watch the show all the time. *Knight Rider, Hulk* and *Brady Bunch* were staples while growing up.

What was your favorite memory from the filming?
I remember playing catch with the football outside the Brady house with Chris Knight, Barry Williams and Jerry Houser, which was really cool. I also remember how everyone was a bunch of pranksters. There were constantly jokes being played on the cast members.

How was it working with Barry?
It was amazing. He was really sweet and really supportive with me being a young actor. He spoke with my mom a lot about being a young actor and what I should watch for and make sure I never fall into. They talked a lot about SAG and child actor's rights. He was very protective. I was also getting over strep throat as I was filming, so I was still pretty weak during most of the project and Robert Reed and Florence Henderson were especially sweet in taking care of me and making sure I was comfortable and had water, etc. in between takes.

Do you remember any funny incidents on the set?
Off the top of my head, no, but, as I said, I just remember us having to do a lot of takes on and off because there would be a lot of goofing around and trying to make people laugh during their big monologues. Especially at the final dinner scene where everyone confessed something. We probably did

that scene twenty-plus times because everyone was trying to get everyone to mess up.

Why didn't you return for *The Bradys* series?
At the time I was on a good roll with projects and my agent spoke with the Schwartz's about the storylines and how much the grandkids would really be involved. There was a huge cast and I had to follow my agent's advice that I would be tied up on a series, but not really in many shows. It was a real shame because I really loved the cast and Lloyd was especially sweet to my mom and I really pushing for me to come back because they loved me and wanted to keep all the cast. It was a really tough decision to make.

You're now forever in a "blue" box - how was that to film?
It was really simple to film and a blast. I still watch the show when it comes on every Christmas and laugh my butt off. It is pretty awesome to say, "Yep, I'm a Brady!"

The Bradys – 1990 – TV series
After the success of *A Very Brady Christmas*, the new dramatic series *The Bradys* was green-lit. The show focused on the adult lives of the Brady kids, which included their marriage and families.

In this installment of the Bradys, Maureen McCormick does not return as Marcia; she is replaced by actress Leah Ayres. Jerry Houser (Wally Logan) and Ron Kuhlman (Phillip Covington III) reprised their roles as the husbands of Marcia and Jan. Martha Quinn plays Tracy, who is married to Bobby Brady. Quinn is best known for being a '80s VJay for MTV. The young actor who plays Greg's son, Zack, is Jonathan Taylor Thomas, who went on to play Tim Allen's son on *Home Improvement*.

The opening song of *The Bradys* contains new grown-up lyrics and was sung by Florence Henderson. *The Bradys* was originally to be three two hour movies, but turned into one two-hour movie and four one-hour shows. Sherwood & Lloyd J. Schwartz headed up the writing of the series. The show aired Friday nights at 8:00 p.m., but, sadly, it only ran for six episodes.

Episode 1: Start Your Engines (a.k.a.: The Brady 500)	February 9, 1990
Episode 2: Here We Grow Again (a.k.a.: The Brady 500)	February 9, 1990
Episode 3: A Moving Experience	February 16, 1990
Episode 4: Hat in the Ring	February 23, 1990
Episode 5: Bottom's Up	March 2, 1990
Episode 6: The Party Girls	March 9, 1990

Brady Bunch Home Movies - 1995 – TV Special/DVD release
The original cast comes back to share many never-before-heard stories and share rare footage from their home movies, which they took with the camera Robert Reed gave them all one year. The special was executive produced by Susan Olsen and Lloyd J. Schwartz was supervising producer.

The Brady Bunch Movie – February 16, 1995 - Motion Picture
The Bradys' house is in jeopardy and they need to find $20,000 to keep it. The kids decide to make money and join together to make a musical group and win the $20,000 award. The film exploited all the fun of the show, including "Johnny Bravo," "Marcia, Marcia, Marcia," Cindy's lisp, Mike's motto speeches and the music. The film was written by Lloyd J. Schwartz and produced by his father, Sherwood.

The Brady Bunch Movie was nominated for three awards, including "Best Dance Sequence," at the 1995 MTV Movie Awards. The film racked in over $45 million dollars in box-office receipts.

Brady-gayism

Marcia's best friend is a lesbian who really thinks she's groovy and during the ending credits they even share a kiss!

Jan's school therapist, Mrs. Cummings, is none other than supermodel RuPaul! Now, Jan ,you better work it, girl! Mama RuPaul will help all those Marcia, Marcia, Marcia problems disappear.

Cast Cameos

Christopher Knight plays the lunchroom monitor who helps Peter with a bully.

Barry Williams plays a music executive who Greg goes to sell his music.

Ann B. Davis plays a trucker who picks up the troubled Jan and advises her about being the middle child.

Florence Henderson plays the Bradys' grandmother.

The Very Brady Sequel – August 23, 1996 – Motion Picture

Here comes more sunshine as the theatrical movie Brady family gets entangled in a mess when Carol's dead husband, Roy Martin (Tim Matheson), arrives at the Bradys' front door. But he is an imposter who is only after the family's horse statue, which Carol has donated to be auctioned. After Roy steals the statue back, he kidnaps Carol and flies to Hawaii to sell the statue.

The film once again touchstones the original series by using the infamous storylines as a house of cards, Jan's made-up boyfriend, Greg moving into the attic, going to Hawaii and the cursed tabu statue.

The film brought over $21 million dollars at the box office and Sherwood & Lloyd Schwartz were on board as producers.

Brady Note: This is the first time that Carol's husband's name, Roy Martin, was used. During the original series, it was considered taboo to be divorced.

Brady-gayism

The whole Brady family wants to be "gay" – well, not "gay" in the sense of the word today, meaning two people of the same sex getting it on ... they want to be "gay" as in the Webster Dictionary: "1 a: happily excited : merry <in a gay mood> b: keenly alive and exuberant : having or inducing high spirits."

RuPaul returns as Mrs. Cummings and tries to help Jan with her problems poolside as RuPaul's daughters are just like the Brady girls except it's all about "Moshe, Moshe, Moshe!"

Greg and Marcia keep having something come up as their sexuality is peeked between the twosome as they live together in the attic.

House Guests:

Rosie O'Donnell and Zsa Zsa Gabor play Beverly Hills elite.

David Spade creates Carol's new look as the flamboyant hairdresser.

Barbara Eden shows up in her iconic role from *I Dream of Jennie* as the first wife of Mike Brady.

Growing Up Brady – May 21, 2000 – TV Special/DVD Release

The film was based on Barry Williams' book, *Growing Up Brady*. The film was based on Barry's memories of filming the series and his crushes on Maureen and Florence.

Adam Brody portrays Barry and Kaley Cuoco plays Maureen. Mike Lookinland does a cameo as a cameraman and his own son, Scott, plays the role of Bobby. Williams plays himself and narrates the film.

Pop-Up Brady – July 18, 2001 – Nick at Night
Some of the episodes of *The Brady Bunch* got the VH1 "Pop-up" treatment, meaning during the show many pop-up notes would show up on the screen. The "Pop-up" originally was done to videos on VH1, but then branched out into TV shows.

Pop-up episodes:
#1 The Honeymoon
#43 Our Son, the Man
#59 Her Sister's Shadow
#61 Getting Davy Jones
#64 Big Little Man
#66 Dough-RE-mi
#96 Adios, Johnny Bravo
#106 The Cincinnati Kids
#117 The Hair-Brained Scheme

The Brady Bunch in the White House – November 29, 2002 – FOX - TV Movie
After Bobby finds a winning lottery ticket and family can't find the owner, Mike decides to give the money to a home for homeless architects and their families. The gesture brings the Bradys to the White House, where Mike gets nominated for the Vice Presidency. After a scandal, Mike is bumped to President with Carol as Vice President and the family takes over the White House.

The movie included many episode situations, including the broken vase, slumber party, wallet found. The film was written by Lloyd J. Schwartz and Hope Juber.

The Brady Bunch 35th Anniversary Reunion Special: Still Brady After All These Years – September 26, 2004 – TVLand

Actress Jenny McCarthy hosted the special, which ran on TVLand. All the remaining Bradys took part in the special. The special was part of a three-day marathon of *The Brady Bunch*, which ran from September 25-27 and included original and Pop-up episodes.

The Brady Bunch Cast Back in Hawaii – June 19, 2005

Five of the original Brady cast, Florence Henderson, Christopher Knight, Mike Lookinland, Susan Olsen, Barry Williams, return to Hawaii with special guest Don Ho to chat about the show.

My Fair Brady – 2005-2007 – TV reality series – E!

Show follows Christopher Knight and his bride-to-be, Adrianne Curry, the first-ever crowned *America's Next Top Model*. Cameras follow the twosome as Curry wants a commitment from Christopher.

The Brady Bunch: Coming Together Under One Roof - 2005- Paramount DVD release

The special is a bonus feature on Paramount's season one DVD. Producer Sherwood Schwartz narrates the documentary.

A Very Brady Musical – 2008 – Stage Production – Los Angeles, CA

In the new musical, the kids overhear Carol and Mike reading a script and believe their parents are going to divorce. After talking with Alice, the kids decided that they need to raise money to have Dr. Anonymous counsel their parents. All the kids take on jobs to make money, but their innocent Brady minds get them all thrown into jail. When the kids are away, Mike and Carol have some hot and kinky sexy. The kids are cleared and it's a sun-shiny day again in Brady world.

Lloyd J. Schwartz has revamped the show into a stage musical with the whole gang and great music. The show had the world premiere on June 6, 2008, with special guest Christopher Knight. Other cast members dropped by during the Los Angeles, CA, run, including Florence Henderson, Barry Williams, Maureen McCormick, and Susan Olsen.

The show will be touring around America, so check out www.averybradymusical.com.

Brady Note: In the musical, the horse statue was how the Carol and Mike first met, when they both wanted to buy it. Yet, the statue in the *Very Brady Sequel* film had no value to Carol so she donates it to an auction.

groovy tip!

The Very Brady Musical won six ADA Valley League Theater Awards for "Best Original Production - Comedy, Drama or Musical," "Best Choreography," "Lighting Design" and "Best Original Play - Lloyd J. Schwartz and Hope Juber." & "Best Director of a Musical - Lloyd J. Schwartz."

A Brady Chat with Hope Juber

Hope Juber is the daughter of show creator Sherwood Schwartz, but she acted on the series playing Rachel, Greg Brady's girlfriend, for two episodes, "Greg Gets Grounded" and "The Big Bet." She also played one of Marcia's best friends, "Jenny," in "The Slumber Caper," and was seen in the final episode, "The Hair-Brained Scheme," as Gretchen.

She later worked continually on Brady shows, including *The Brady Brides* and co-wrote the TV film *The Brady Bunch in the White House* and the newest musical, *A Very Brady Musical*, with her brother Lloyd.

Keep up with Hope and all her upcoming projects at http://www.hopejuber.com/

How was it working with Barry Williams?
It was great. He was a buddy of mine and we got along really well.

Did you have a crush on him?
Actually, no, I did not have a crush on Barry. I went for a different type, the cute English guitarist.

How was it shooting your date scenes with Barry and Mike in "The Big Bet"?
That was a blast. Mike Lookinland was really fun to work with. It was so nice to have a character that came back more than once. Barry and Mike were professional, but they were kids and I was a kid, too. It was a fun family set to work on and everyone felt very comfortable with each other.

How was it working with the frogs in "Greg Gets Grounded"?
It took a long time because frogs don't necessarily cooperate. There was this contraption built above the car where the guy had a sack full of frogs he would drop on my head. It got icky at times because of the frogs. I don't know if they were wet or what but occasionally frog juice would rain down on me and they would have to dry my hair again.

How was it filming the "The Slumber Caper" episode?
There were a lot of kids there and a lot I actually knew because Florence Henderson's daughter, Barbara, was there and Robert Reed's daughter, Karen, was there, too. I was really good friends with Barbara and still am. Maureen, Barbara and I used to hang out a lot together as friends so the filming had the actual feel of a real teenage sleepover party because we were all buddies.

How was it growing up so close to the Bradys?

For me, it was different. I was not actually a Brady, but they were a big part of my home family life. Not only was my dad was involved with it so extensively, but my brother also was there. There were the four Schwartz kids and there were these six other Bradys and there were as many pictures of them on the walls as there were of us. They were this alternate family which was very perfect in a lot of ways. Sometimes that kind of juxtaposed with going though adolescence and feeling not so perfect.

How was it writing the new musical, *A Very Brady Musical*, with your brother, Lloyd?

That was *wonderful*! That was so much fun. We had such a great time doing that production. Every couple of minutes we would say, "Let's throw in this reference," or "How about this episode?" and "I always wanted to have this character say this, let's go for it."

We got to use all of our experience and our pent-up feelings about the Bradys and that whole scenario just to have the ultimate in fun with those characters and get them to do things and say things we always wanted them to do.

In the musical, can you tell me how the story about the Brady horse statue came about?

We wanted to establish a connection. There was never any proposed way of how Mike and Carol met. We wanted to give them a way they met, which incorporated something classic Brady. So we figured if we put them in a swap meet and they see this horse statue, which they both loved, and their eyes meet over both wanting the statue; it really incorporated not only them and their personality, but you take this iconic horse and have it represent their meeting, love for each other and their commonality. It seemed such a fun way to go.

What was your favorite incarnation?
I have fondness for a couple of them. *The Brady Brides*, of course, because during *Brady Brides* was when I met my husband. That was the first time I jumped into being a writer. I started writing on that and very quickly became a story editor, which was a real thrill. *The Brady Bunch in the White House* was exciting, because it was the first movie Lloyd and I wrote together, but the *Brady Musical* probably was the most satisfying because there is something about doing live musical theater when the actors start singing your songs or saying something you think is funny and the audience gets it. There is something very magical about that. *A Very Brady Musical*, I would say, I enjoyed the most out of everything.

The Brady Effects
The Brady Bunch's pop culture effect has been seen in so many gags on TV shows since the series left the air in the '70s. Here are just a handful of very Brady examples.

The Love Boat "Affair on Demand" – 1983 - TV Series
"Brady" is not mentioned, but guest stars Robert Reed's and Florence Henderson's characters mention how they can take a cruise since the kids are all grown up.

Day By Day "A Very Brady Episode" - 1989 - TV series
In the episode, the teenage boy in the family (Christopher Daniel Barnes) dreams he's Chuck Brady and escapes to the Bradys' world after he's yelled at for his poor scholastic habits (he was watching a *Brady* marathon); however, Chuck's dream comes apart when various Bradys begin repeating comments made only a few minutes earlier.

The series starred Linda Kelsey and Courtney Thorne-Smith. Robert Reed and Florence Henderson, Ann B. Davis, Maureen McCormick, Christopher Knight and Michael Lookinland reprise their roles as Bradys in this episode.

Brady Note: Barnes went on to star as Greg in *The Brady Bunch Movie* and *A Very Brady Sequel*.

Free Spirit "The New Secretary" - 1989 – TV series
Robert Reed and Florence Henderson play a couple seeking a divorce in an episode of this short-lived sitcom about a witch (Corinne Bohrer) working as a nanny to a widowed lawyer.

Hi Honey, I'm Home "SRP" 1991 - TV series
The show centers on a black-and-white TV show family which has to live in the real world until they can return to TV. Ann B. Davis makes a guest appearance as Alice Nelson.

Saturday Night Live "Brady Bunch vs. Partridge Family" - 1992 – TV series
In the *SNL* skit Jan joins The Partridge Family but after she finds out they fake sing, the Brady Six and The Partridge Family have a Battle of the Bands. Susan Dey, who played Laurie Partridge, reprises her role in the skit.

MTV Video Awards "A Few Very Brady Good Men" - 1993 – TV Special
Florence Henderson as Carol Brady, in the best role of her life, in a parody of *A Few Good Men* film. Greg (Barry Williams) cross-examines Carol about her cleaning tactics, the grounding of Marcia. This was a segment was a part of the MTV Movie Awards. Christopher Knight and Susan Olsen were also in the parody.

The Family Guy - "Death Has a Shadow" - 1999- TV series
The Griffin Family is watching *The Brady Bunch* on TV. The episode has Jan tattling on Greg about finding a cigarette in his jacket.

The Slmpsons "The Simpsons Spin-off Showcase" - 1997 – TV Series

The episode consists of three "potential spin-offs" of the show, including *The Simpson Family Smile-time Variety Hour*, which showcases a "replacement Lisa" to mimic *The Brady Bunch Variety Hour* "replacement Jan," Geri Reischl.

Unauthorized Brady Bunch: The Final Days –2000 – TV movie

An unauthorized film based on the turmoil of the series. The film mainly focused on the fights between Sherwood Schwartz and Robert Reed. The film was not associated with any of the producers or stars of the show.

That '70s Show "Red Sees Red" - 2000 – TV series

The Formans sit down to watch *The Brady Bunch Variety Hour* as Kitty dreams that the family has their own variety show called *The Forman Bunch Variety Hour*. The show guest stars Shirley Jones, TV mom rival from *The Partridge Family*.

The Family Guy "Emission Impossible" – 2001- TV Series

Stewie mentions "Cousin Oliver" when he compares himself to Bobby Brady while fretting about Lois and Peter's attempts for another child.

ESPN's True Hollywood Story: Tom Brady – 2001- TV Special

The special uncovers that Patriots quarterback star; Tom Brady was really the fourth Brady boy. Tom Brady, Barry Williams, Christopher Knight and Mike Lookinland tell the true story of how Tom was the one who broke Marcia's nose and how concerned they were after he was fired. Now the Brady brothers are very proud of him.

The X-Files "Sunshine Days" 2002 – TV series
Oliver Martin uses his extreme mental abilities to warp the inside of his home to resemble the Brady house, along with embodiments of the Bradys themselves, including Alice.

Robot Chicken: "Mr. & Mrs. Brady" Episode "Suck It" - 2006 – TV series
Carol and Mike kick each other's ass in a parody on the hit film *Mr. & Mrs. Smith*. The twosome kill all the children and begin to have hot steamy sex

That '70s Show "We Will Rock You" - 2006 – TV series
Barry Williams (Jeff) and Christopher Knight (Josh) play the new gay neighbors to Red and Kitty Forman. Red accepts their homosexuality, but after Josh reveals they are Eagles fans, Red kicks them out.

Not The Bradys XXX – 2007 – DVD
Oh no!! The Bradys like you never have seen them before ... having *sex*!!!! Now that is not very Brady! In the film, the kids overhear that Mike has lost an account and the family is financially strapped and the kids decided to take on jobs to help out. Needless to say, the Brady kids get themselves in some very sticky situations. What's most fun about the film is that the storyline really could have been an episode of the series. The film starred Hillary Scott, with special house guest Ron Jeremy as Sam the butcher.

groovy tip!
It became urban legend that the one in curls, Susan Olsen, had done a porn film! Well, Susan *did*, but she only created a movie soundtrack for a friend's '80s XXX film titled *Crocodile Blondee*.

Not The Bradys XXX: Marcia, Marcia, Marcia – 2008 – DVD
Here's the story... the first DVD did so well they made a sequel! When Marcia gets a chance to win a date with teen idol Danny Jones, she recruits the entire family for an amateur singing contest. But first, she has to convince her parents that she didn't send Danny a racy fan letter – complete with a pair of dirty panties! Plus, she has to talk them out of taking a family trip to New Jersey. And then Greg has a little problem in the bathroom – okay a *big* problem!

Another Gay Sequel: Gays Gone Wild – 2008 – Theatrical Film
The end of the film has gossip guru-turned-actor Perez Hilton singing an original song in the famous blue Brady boxes.

Monk "Mr. Monk's Favorite Show" - 2009 - TV Series
Monk is obsessed with an old TV show called "The Cooper Clan." Monk is hired to help find a killer who is after one of the show's stars. This episode plays homage to The Brady Bunch with parodying the shows story line situations, family characters including the dog, and the set all the way down to the stairway and of course "Adrian, Adrian, Adrian!"

groovy tip!
Finally, it happened: two Brady boys kiss!! Barry Williams and Christopher Knight, playing a gay couple, locked lips on *That '70s Show*.

Barry Williams and Christopher Knight meet their fans at the Hollywood Collectors Show in Burbank, CA. (photo © Joey Marshall)

Chapter Five: Why We Love The Bradys

Opening Theme

Who could forget the opening song for *The Brady Bunch*? "Here's a story..." We all can sing it. The song was the brainchild of the show's producer, Sherwood Schwartz. During the first season, it was sung by The Peppermint Trolley Company. When the show was picked up for the second season, the producers had the Brady kids sing the opening. Little did they know that having them sing the opening would push the kids to become recording stars, producing five records and a touring schedule.

Sherwood also developed the nine-piece opening because TV was a close medium and the best way to introduce nine people was with close-up shots. He created this blue checkerboard idea to introduce the six kids, two parents and Alice. For each season a new blue box was filmed to reflect the growing family.

Today, *The Brady Bunch* opening song and blue boxes have found a new life on YouTube as many fans have made homemade show openings, including "The Jedi Bunch" for *Star Wars* fans; "The Matey Bunch," to encourage others to spay and neuter pets, and "Getting Laid A Bunch," about really ugly people getting trashed and having a orgy.

Wherever you are around the world, if you see that checkerboard and hear that music, regardless what language it might be sung in ... you know you're in Brady World!

The Hair & Clothing

The girls with hair of gold and boys with hair of brown, they were the perfect American family! Who could go wrong with Marcia's perfectly combed, long, flowing hair, which she took care of daily with 100 brushes? Jan, with her straight hair with curly-curls that framed her face as did her glasses. Cindy's signature curls of gold were just the most perfect, and then were later turned into pigtails. The girls got their wonderful locks from Carol, whose bob-cut with a bottom flip was soon all the rage.

The boys' hairstyles were classic male American looks, but after their trip to Hawaii the boys' hair went wild! The weather in Hawaii brought the curls out in Mike, Greg and Peter's hair. From that point, the men's hair was curly, curly, curly! If you really want curls, check out Jan's wig - it was far out.

The Brady clothing reflected the grooviest looks during the first years. The colors were very bold with dominate colors, but as the seventies began to come into full swing the Bradys began to wear paisley patterns with bellbottoms. Don't forget "hang-ten" t-shirts, which even Mike Brady was seen wearing.

The one fun thing to check out while watching the series is that the kids wore the same outfits numerous times and kids' clothing even became hand-me-downs. But don't forget the best fashion statement of all: Alice's blue work dress.

The Family Wheels

The all-American family has to drive an all-American car. What better choice for the Bradys than driving Chrysler? Except maybe driving Chevrolet during the final season.

Mike Brady vehicles:
Pilot: 1968 Dodge Polara convertible
Season 1 & 2:   1969 Plymouth Fury III
Season 3:   1971 Plymouth Barracuda convertible
Season 4:   1972 Plymouth Barracuda (updated version of the 1971) convertible
Season 5:   1973 Chevrolet Caprice convertible – color red
                        This season was the only year that Mike did not drive a Chrysler car. (#50-52)
                        License plate: TEL 635

Carol Brady vehicles:
Season 2:   1970 Plymouth Satellite wagon
Season 3:   1971 Plymouth Satellite wagon
                        The Bradys used this car for their trip to the Grand Canyon.

Greg Brady vehicles:
Season 3:   1957 Chrysler dark-blue convertible
                        Greg buys this hunk of junk for $100 in "The Wheel Dealer" (#53), which he tries to rebuild. Today, the car is worth a pretty penny.

The *real* Brady home, located in Los Angeles, California. The current owners built the fence to keep fans off the yard. (photo © Mike Pingel)

The Brady Home

The split-level home was selected for its modest middle-American look. One challenge for the production crew was making the split level look like was a roomy two-story dwelling. When they filmed the exterior shots of the real home, a window was placed on the side to make it look like it had a second floor.

Interesting to find out that exterior shots of *The Brady Bunch* house is an actual house located in the residential area of San Fernando Valley, CA. Over the years, the appearance has changed with an added iron fence and overgrown shrubbery.

Exteriors of the original house were filmed once again for the TV movie *A Very Brady Christmas* and for the short-lived TV series *The Bradys*. When time came for *The Brady Bunch* feature film, a new façade was built, since the original home no longer looked the same.

groovy tip!

Mike Brady's house in the pilot episode, "The Honeymoon," was a different home. It was seen only once, in the pilot. The home was a white one-story home; it was felt that, with the large family, the home should be two stories.

Groovy Websites

Need to know more about the Bradys? Well, here are some online destinations for everything Brady Bunch!

Brady World:	http://www.bradyworld.com
The Brady Kids:	http://www.geocities.com/brady_kids2001/index.html
The Brady Bunch Shrine:	http://www.bradybunchshrine.com
Brady Residence:	http://www.bradyresidence.com/
The Canonical Brady Bunch Episode Guide	http://www.nyx.net/~thill/brady.html

A Brady Chat with Wendy Winans

Wendy Winans shares her passion with the fans of the world with her hugely informative and beloved site, **www.BradyWorld.com**

What is the number one question fans write in about *The Brady Bunch*?

The most asked question by fans and non-fans at Brady World is whether or not Tom Brady, quarterback for the New England Patriots, was truly on the show and was he edited out for throwing the infamous football at Marcia. This question comes from a spoof that ESPN did back in Tom Brady's rookie year (2001) about him being a lost Brady. The clip was in the fashion of a *True Hollywood Story* expose that stated that there were originally four Brady boys, one being Tom, and that he threw the infamous football that hit Marcia, which the directors did not like, therefore fired him and edited out all references to him. This was intended to be a joke. Since that time, whenever the New England Patriots have made it to the Super Bowl, which has been often, ESPN digs out the old clip and again people far and wide wonder if it's really true. My typical response is to say that it was, of course, a spoof and that let's not forget that the Bradys are a fictional family, whereas Tom Brady is a real person, and the most convincing evidence that this could not be possible was that Tom Brady was born August 3, 1977, three years after *The Brady Bunch* went off the air.

How many fans visit your site?

Brady World receives, on average, 800 visitors per day. The age range for fans runs from about five years old to about 60 years old. I think this statistic shows the longevity of the show and that each new generation finds something about the show endearing.

How did you become a huge fan of the series?

My love for the show started back when I was about five years old. As a young child, I started a scrapbook, cut out photographs from old teen magazines I found at flea markets and kept track of the reunions over the years. I also bought a lot of the merchandise as a child and never gave it away. However, the change from average fan to the current success with Brady World starts back in 1995 when I became interested in the web and wanted to design a website. I began reading tutorials on web design and looked at other sites and decided to make a website about the *Brady Bunch* because I had a great deal of knowledge about the show. There was only one other site on the subject at the time and the designer of that site has since lost interest. When Brady World first started it was a relatively small website and had only a few areas for fans to visit. However, over the years, with gathering more knowledge, making contact and gaining the respect of many of the original cast members, Brady World has grown into a world-recognized site on the subject of *The Brady Bunch* and its cast. My personal interest and collection has also grown as a result of the web, because of websites like eBay. My thorough collection (which includes a coveted Kitty-Karry-All doll, the complete trading-card series and board game) has been, in the past, loaned-out to the "Rock & Roll Hall of Fame" in Cleveland, OH, and also to "Toy Town" in Aurora, NY, so that others could enjoy the nostalgia of the show.

What was your favorite episode of the original series?
My favorite episode of *The Brady Bunch* is a first-season episode entitled "Father of the Year." I think this episode is a wonderful example of why people continue to enjoy the show. This episode shows how a family should work through its problems. It touched on the issue of a blended family, it focused on a child breaking the rules, how the child was punished and that in the end a lesson was learned and a family grew stronger. In the episode, Marcia enters Mike Brady in a local newspaper contest for "Father of the Year." In trying to hide her secret, she gets into trouble and is denied the opportunity to go on a family trip. Even though she gets angry and originally believes that she is being treated unfairly, in the end, her love for her new stepfather and her understanding that because she broke the rules, despite her reasons, she deserved to be punished, led to a happy ending when Mike wins the contest and their bond of father-daughter is stronger than ever.

If you were to write a Brady episode, what situation would you put the Bradys in?
I have thought about this question for several weeks now and I have not been able to come up with a comedic episode that I would write for the younger cast. However, I still believe that a reunion should be done dealing

with the death of Mike Brady. I feel we have learned so many lessons from the Bradys over the last 40 years that the final lesson should be about how a family comes together in support when the patriarch dies. How the kids rally around Carol in support. How we explain to the grandkids about death, etc. Yes, the episode would be very tragic and sad, but death is a part of life

Chapter Six:
The Very Brady Characters

Here is a little story of each character from background pulled from the original series. Sometimes not all the information links up.

Michael Paul "Mike" Brady - "Father"
Mike Brady was married and had three children, all boys, Greg, Peter and Bobby. His wife passed away. In 1969, he remarried, to Carol, who had three daughters.

Mike attended Freemont High School and "Bobo" was his high-school crush. "Hot Lips" was his nickname in high school. During his high school years, he stole a rival mascot and was suspended. Later, he attended Norton College. He became a sought-after architect.

He is in his late thirties, likes to golf and loves olives never had the mumps, and can make a mean soufflé. He is best known for his lectures and solid advice.

Mike later became a senior partner in the architect firm and ran for city council.

Carol Ann Tyler Martin Brady - "Mother"
Carol went to the Westdale Elementary High School, where her children

now attend. She even had the same teacher, Ms. Whitfield. "Twinkles" is Carol's pet name by her high-school sweetheart, Tank Gates, the football quarterback and senior-year boyfriend. She attended State University and dreamed of becoming a photographer.

While growing up, she use to fish with her father. Her grandmother's strawberry preserve won four blue ribbons.

Makes sculptures and is avid at needlepoint. She is a beautiful singer and shares her talent with Marcia's school and at church.

She divorced her first husband, Roy Martin, with whom she had three girls, Marcia, Jan and Cindy. She remarried, to Mike Brady, in 1969.

After the kids moved out, Carol persuade a career in real estate

Gregory "Greg" Brady "Oldest Brother"

Greg is fourteen when Mike married Carol in 1969. He attended Fillmore Junior High School and then Westdale High School. Joined the football team in high school and was number #23 and played first string. Greg was known "old sliver tongue" because he talks so smooth to the girls. He also plays golf and surfs. Is a photographer and is interested in filmmaking.

He was the big man on campus with the girls. He keeps his hot male figure with surfing. His first job was an office boy at Mike's architect office, then a delivery boy for Sam the butcher and was the lead singer of The Brady Six! (And the Sliver Platter.) Stardom almost happened when he was picked to be singer "Johnny Bravo."

Later, Greg became an obstetrician and married Nora and has one son, Kevin. When his brother Bobby is paralyzed, he wanted to return to school to help him.

Marcia Brady - "Oldest Sister"

Marcia was 12 in 1969 when her mother married Mike Brady. While at Fillmore Juror High School Marcia was class president and on the debating team, placed first in the swim meet and editor of the school newspaper.

She is good at volleyball, won the "Outstanding Citizenship Award and received first place in an art show.

Begins to attend the Westdale High School in the fall of 1972 and joined the ceramic club. In high school she tried out for the cheerleading team.

Marcia's other interests are ballet and she is the President of the Davy Jones Fan Club. Her first job was at an ice shop, a job she lost to Jan.

Marcia became a fashion designer. She married Wally Logan and had two children, Mickey and Jessica. At one point, she was a stay-at-home mom and later opened her own catering business with Wally's sisters.

Peter Brady - "Middle Brother"
Peter attends Fillmore Junior High School, where he plays the role of Benedict Arnold in the school play. During his time in high school, he was part of the science club and builds a volcano. Kerry Hathaway was his first love. His other interests lie in painting, playing baseball and photography. He also taught himself to be a magician. His first job was at the bike shop, and then he briefly worked at the ice cream scoop shop with Marcia.

He wanted to be a doctor, but instead, when he grew up, he joined the military for a while, and then became an administrative assistant. He is currently still single.

Jan Brady - "Middle Sister"
While attending Fillmore Junior High School she was in charge of the scenery for the play *George Washington* and was voted "most popular" in middle school.

Her other interests are ballet (which she drops out of) and wants to be a nurse when she grows up. She occasionally hears voices and enjoys wearing wigs. Her first job was at the ice cream shop, where she replaced Marcia.

While in college she met and married her professor, Phillip Covington III. The couple did have a brief separation, but got back together and adopted a Korean girl, Patty.

Robert "Bobby" Brady - "Youngest Brother"
Bobby was seven when his father married Carol. He attends the Clinton Ave Elementary. He is great at sports, at shooting pool and dreams of being a pool champion. Also on his want list of things to do are astronaut, football player and wrestler. He is also a teeter-totter champion. His football hero is Joe Namath, who he got to meet.

He has a pet hamster named Henrietta. He also had to endure braces and his hero as a child was Jesse James, until he discovers he was not a very nice guy.

Bobby became a well-known race car driver, but was paralyzed after an accident. He opened a business venture with his brother and married Tracy.

Cynthia "Cindy" Brady - "Youngest Sister"
Cindy was seven when her mother married Mike Brady. She is best known for her tattling and snooping expertise. She is also known for her wonderful curly locks and was graced with wearing braces.

She attends Clinton Avenue Grammar Elementary and has a crush on 12-year-old Joey Finton.

In Cindy's spare time she takes ballet and plays jacks. She is a huge fan and wants to be the new of Shirley Temple in films. She and her brother Bobby found greatness when they made a world record with teeter-totter.

She plans to grow up to be a model and lady wrestler. But, when she grew up, she became a deejay and had a romance with her boss. She is currently unmarried.

Alice Nelson Franklin - "The house keeper"
She attended school at PS34 and PS43, although she was not sure which one came first. She had the acting bug and was an actor in the Pilgrim Festival and the public schools she attended. She played the role of Julius Caesar in her high-school senior play. Her talents also win her a commercial jingle contest.

Alice never learned how to drive a car and so she is quite familiar with the city bus transportation system. She has a pet gold fish "Herman," who is pregnant. She was originally the housekeeper for Mike Brady and his boys and continued working for the couple after they married in 1969.

One her most prize family possession is a cameo, which is passed onto to Jan Brady. She is a very good cook for the family; her aunt's strawberry preserves won six blue ribbons. Alice has an ongoing relationship with Sam "The Butcher" Franklin, the twosome met at a dance when he was in the army. Sam courts her with wonderful pieces of meat from his shop and at her cousin's wedding he asks Alice to marry him. It's not until later do the twosome get hitched.

Visiting the Bradys

One can visit Schwartz, Henderson and Davis, not at their home but on the shiny Hollywood Walk of Fame in Hollywood, California. Each of them have been bestowed the honor of a star on the Walk of Fame. Here are the addresses to go say 'Hi.'

Sherwood Schwartz	6541 Hollywood Boulevard, Hollywood, CA
Florence Henderson	7060 Hollywood Boulevard, Hollywood, CA
Ann B. Davis	7048 Hollywood Boulevard, Hollywood, CA

94 **The Brady Bunch**

Geri & Susan are still best buddies! (photo courtesy of Geri Reischl)

The Family Tree

Honorary Bradys:

Alan Melvin "Sam: the Butcher" *The Brady Bunch*
Melvin played the love interest with the Bradys' housekeeper, Alice. He ran the butcher shop and always gave Alice a good price on his meat! The twosome had a relationship which spanned the series and spin-offs. Alice mentions in "The Elopement" that they are engaged, but in later episodes Alice is still trying to pin him down. During the spin-offs, Sam and Alice finally marry. One would think Sam was on the original series weekly, but he was only seen in eight episodes, but his name was mentioned many times. Sam was also an avid bowler.

    Melvin had a long acting career. He had recurring roles on many series, including *The Phil Silvers Show, All in the Family* and *Archie Bunker's Place*. He also lent his voice to numerous cartoon shows, including *The Flintstones, Smurfs, Popeye,* and *Yo Yogi!* Melvin passed way on January 21, 2008.

Robbie Rist "Cousin Oliver Martin" *The Brady Bunch*
In 1973 Robbie Rist was integrated into the role of Cousin Oliver in the final five episodes of the series in the hopes of keeping the younger viewing audience. Rist got the role after being one of the front runners for the hopeful Brady spin-off series, *Kelly's Kids*. The cute kid with the wire-rimmed glasses could not save the show, which was not going to return.

    Rist went on to play recurring roles in *The Bionic Woman, Galactica 1980* and many *Afterschool Specials*. He won the role of David Baxter, the son of Ted Baxter (Ted Knight), on the final season of *The Mary Tyler Moore Show*. In 1981 he nominated for the "Best Young Artist" award for his work in the TV movie *ABC Weekend Specials: The Big Hex of Little Lulu*. He works at voicing cartoon characters in such projects as *Teenage Mutant*

Ninja Turtles, *Naruto* and *Zatch Bell!* Check out his website at: http://www.robbierist.com.

A Brady Chat with Robbie Rist

How did you land the gig on The Brady Bunch?
I tried out for the Bradys' spin-off television show called *Kelly's Kids*. It was going to star Ken Berry. I went to the last callback and they were ready to go with me. It came down to the fact that Ken Berry was a brunet and I was a blond, so they went with another kid and there was never a spin-off. Then the show had this character [Cousin Oliver] they called me in for. 500 other kids read for the part and I got it.

Where you a fan of the show prior?
Only so much. I was more of a *Six Million Dollar Man* guy.

What do you think about the "Cousin Oliver Syndrome"?
I don't think anybody had any idea the show was going to be like this. Here we are almost 40 years later and it's still around and it has deep roots in the culture; notwithstanding the character I did. It's become infamous [Cousin Oliver] for things that are not good anymore. How crazy is that? It has nothing to do with me. It was a character on a TV show now used as a phrase to describe other things that have gone bad.

groovy tip!
"Cousin Oliver Syndrome" is named after Robbie Rist's character on *The Brady Bunch*. The phrase is used in the television industry to describe a show with losing ratings which brings in a young child in hopes to boost the viewing audience. Most of the time this does not work and the show is canceled.

Cousin Oliver has even been mentioned in *The Onion*, a weekly satirical newspaper, as to being invited to join the White House for Clinton's final term to increase the administration's popularity. The oh-so-cute Cousin Oliver was also rumored to have joined the White House for both of President George W. Bush's terms, according to Robbie Rist.

When did you find out that the fifth season was the end?
When the end of summer rolled around and they told us it wasn't going to be renewed.

How was it working with the cast?
It was great. They had been there for a while and I was nine. I always have been a gregarious dude, so I got along with everybody. For six weeks it was a pretty fun job.

Any fun stories from the set?
Susan Olsen split my lip on the teeter-totter. If you look at some of my later episodes, all of a sudden there is this huge thing on my lip. We were bouncing on the teeter-totter. Susan was bigger than me and bounced it hard and I sailed over the handlebars and slid on my face all the way down to her. It's pretty funny.

What is your favorite gig ever?
I like to work. I don't care what I'm working on. When on-camera work dried up for me, I went into voiceovers. Every job is my favorite job.

What are you doing now?
A lot of stuff, I just a produced a movie called *Stump the Band* (http://www.stumptheband.com) and I'm producing and playing with a lot of bands (www.myspace.com/robbierist). I'm also working on a book for parents

and kids who want to get into show business. The book will show how to do it right and for the right reasons. I'm also doing voiceovers here and there. I consider myself an entertainment guy.

What did you take away from being a part of the Brady Bunch?

I know for a fact that I wouldn't have whatever career I had if it not been for *The Brady Bunch*. The show was such a part of the culture zeitgeist. I'm known for it everywhere. I've been to foreign countries and have been recognized for *The Brady Bunch*. That's pretty crazy. It was a cool six-week job, which turned into something I'm still talking about 40 years later.

Replacement Brady Girls:

During the next few recreations of the series the Brady girls took turns not returning to the revisited series. Here the story of each replacement Bradys.

Geri Reischl "Jan" *The Brady Bunch Hour*

Geri was hired to play Jan Brady for the one-hour variety hour. Geri became known as the "Replacement Jan" and the "Fake Jan" and became a cult icon. *The Simpsons* even used a fake "Lisa" in their episode, *The Simpson Family Smile-Time Variety Hour*. Reischl had parts in *The Brotherhood of Satan* and *I Dismember Mama*. She was also in the running for the lead in the horror classic *The Exorcist*.

Geri is currently working on a talk show called *MY P.I.M.P. TV*, with Ernest Thomas (from *What's Happening!!* and *Everybody Hates Chris*) and also with a comedienne named Pebbles. It is edgy and raw. Not your average talk show.

Jennifer Runyon "Cindy" *A Very Brady Christmas*
Jennifer took over the role of Cindy Brady for the holiday film *A Very Brady Christmas*, but after the film spawned the series *The Bradys*, Susan Olsen reprised her role. Runyon is best known for her role as Gwendolyn Pierce in the TV series *Charles in Charge* and was seen in the films *Ghostbusters* and *The Falcon and the Snowman*.

Leah Ayres "Marcia" *The Bradys*
A busy TV actress of the '80s, Leah stepped into the shoes of Marcia Brady for *The Bradys*, which was a spin-off series from the hit film *A Very Brady Christmas*. Ayres is the co-founder of Imaginazium, LLC.

Extended Brady Tree:
During the following series and films, the Brady family grew. Here is a list of the Bradys' extended spouses and families.

Jerry Houser ... Wally Logan *The Brady Brides, A Very Brady Christmas, The Bradys*
Houser played Wally, who married Marcia, in *The Brady Brides* and reprised his role throughout two more Brady creations. He went on to do voices for numerous animated films, such as Disney's *Aladdin* and *Charlotte's Web 2: Wilbur's Great Adventure*.

G.W. Lee ... Mickey Logan *A Very Brady Christmas*
Lee played Mickey, Marcia's son.

Michael Melby ... Mickey Logan *The Bradys*
Melby played Mickey Logan on the series *The Bradys* and replaced G.W. Lee, the original Mickey.

Jaclyn Bernstein ... Jessica Logan *A Very Brady Christmas* & *The Bradys*

Bernstein played Jessica Logan, the daughter of Marcia. She continued to work on TV in guest roles on *Blossom* and *Step by Step*, among others.

Ron Kuhlman "Philip Covington III" *The Brady Brides, A Very Brady Christmas* & *The Bradys*

Kuhlman played Philip, who married Jan, in *The Brady Brides* and reprised his role throughout two more Brady creations. He's had guest roles on *Melrose Place* and *Profiler*, among others.

Valerie Ick ... Patty Covington *The Bradys*

Ick played Patty Covington, Jan's adopted daughter.

Caryn Richman ... Nora Brady *A Very Brady Christmas*

Richman played Nora, the wife of Greg. In 1991, she took over the role of Lauren Fenmore on *The Young and the Restless* and starred in the short-lived series *Hollywood Safari*.

Zachary Bostrom ... Kevin Brady *A Very Brady Christmas*

Bostrom played Kevin, the son of Greg. He continues to work with guest star roles on *Will & Grace, CSI* and *Close to Home*.

Jonathan Taylor Thomas... Kevin Brady *The Bradys*

Thomas replaced Zachary Bostrom as Greg's son, Kevin, in the series *The Bradys*. He went to play Randy Taylor on the hit TV series *Home Improvement*.

Martha Quinn - Tracy Brady *The Bradys*

Quinn played Tracy, who married Bobby. She went on to be one of the original VJs on MTV, and currently has a radio show, *Gods of the Big '80s*, on Sirius.

Chapter Seven:
The Brady Stories

Season One
ABC; 1969-1970
Friday 8:00 p.m.

Episode 1: The Honeymoon (The Pilot)
Written by: Sherwood Schwartz
Directed by: John Rich
Airdate: September 26, 1969
Mike and Carol decide to get married. At the ceremony, the family pets, Tiger and Fluffy, ransack the wedding. The happy couple arrives at their honeymoon destination and can't stop thinking about kids. They decide to return home to pick up the kids, the pets and Alice.

Brady Tip:
Alice was already working for Mr. Brady.
Fluffy the cat is the girls' pet.
Tiger the dog is the boys' pet.
The show opens with *The Brady Bunch* In COLOR .
Carol's wedding dress matches the tablecloths.

Cast Note:
While filming this episode, Susan Olsen told producer Sherwood Swartz that she was smart enough to know that butterflies did not fly down your stomach and she did not want to say that line.

Episode #2: Dear Libby

Written: Lois Hire
Directoe: John Rich
Airdate: October 3, 1969

Believing that the letter featured in the "Dear Libby" column is about their family, the kids become overly polite and finish their chores without being reminded. After the kids tell Mike and Carol about the column, they begin to think that each other wrote the letter. Dear Libby drops by the house and informs them the letter came from a family in Kingsford, Illinois.

Brady Pen Names
Greg: Guilt Complex; Marcia: Desperately Worried; Peter: Down in the Mouth; Jan: Real Frantic; Bobby: Feeling Awful; Cindy: Kitty Karry-All; Alice: Innocent Bystander

Brady Tidbits;
Carol loves doing needlepoint.
Mike likes the *Peanuts* comic strip.

Episode #3 Eenie, Meenie, Mommy Daddy

Writer: Joanna Lee
Director John Rich
Airdate: October 10, 1969

Cindy gets the lead in the school play, *The Fairy Princess*. When the seating at the theater is over booked, each student only gets one ticket. Poor Cindy has to figure out which parent she has to uninvited to the event. In the end, a special showing of the play is given to the entire Brady clan.

Brady Tip:
Cindy goes to Dixie Canyon School.
Bobby's real name is Robert.
Marcia wants to have Faye Dunaway's nose.
Bobby's turtle is named Herman.

Brady House Guest:
Brian Foster "Elf"
Foster is best known for the role of Chris Partridge from the rival show *The Partridge Family*.

Episode #4 Alice Doesn't Live Here Anymore

Writer: Paul West
Director: John Rich
Airdate: October 17, 1969
When Carol feels that she is not needed by the boys, Alice has them talk to Carol about their problems instead of her. After a short time period, Alice begins to feel that she is no longer needed and decides to leave the Bradys. The family goes into OPERATION: ALICE to show her how much they really need her.

Brady Tip:
The boys get a telescope.
Alice has been working for Mike Brady for seven years, four months, and thirteen days.

Episode 5: Katchoo

Written: William Cowley
Directed: John Rich
Airdate: October 24, 1969

Jan is having a severe allergic reaction to Tiger, the family dog. As the children say their goodbyes, it is learned that Jan is actually allergic to Tiger's new flea powder.

Brady Tip:

Mike likes his tuna salad made with tuna, chopped eggs and pickled relish. Mike was known as the Checkered Champion of Chestnut Avenue.

Episode 6: A Clubhouse is Not a Home

Written: Skip Webster
Directed: John Rich
Airdate: October 31, 1969

It's the "Battle of the Bradys!" as the kids get into a rumble over sharing their stuff with each other. As the girls prepare to build their own clubhouse, they realize that they need the boys' assistance to complete the project.

Tidbit:

"Project Brady Bunch" is what Mike Brady refers to the merging of all the kids.
Greg calls the girls "Dragon Ladies."
Mike is a member of the National Guard.

Brady Moral:

The importance of sharing and respecting each other's privacy!

EPISODE 7: Kitty Karry-All Is Missing

Writer: Al Schwartz & Bill Freedman
Director: John Rich
Airdate: November 7, 1969

Cindy's Kitty Karry-All doll has gone missing. Everyone thinks that Bobby is behind the prank and believes that he is guilty. They eventually find out that Tiger is the one who ran off with the doll.

Brady Tidbits
Mike plays golf.

Brady Pantry:
Alice is making a pot roast for dinner.

A Brady Moral:
Mike gives the kids some advice by telling them that someone is presumed innocent before proven guilty.

EPISODE 8: A-Camping We Go

Written: Herbert Finn & Alan Dinehart
Directed: Oscar Rudolph
Airdate: November 14, 1969

The family ventures off on their first camping trip together, which brings the kids closer together.

Brady Tidbits:
Alice flunked psychology in school.
Alice punctured the air mattress with her hair curls.

Episode 9: Sorry, Right Number
Written: Ruth Brooks Flippen
Directed: George Chan
Airdate: November 21, 1969
The Bradys decide to get a second phone line. Upon receiving an outrageous phone bill, Mike decides to put a pay phone in the house to keep costs down.

Brady Tidbit:
First episode we meet Sam Franklin, the Butcher, played by Allan Melvin.
Greg has an autographed picture of Raquel Welch.
Peter's best friend is Jerry.
Carol is best friends with Martha.

Episode 10: Every Boy Does It Once
Writer: Lois and Arnold Peyser
Director: Oscar Rudolph
Airdate: December 5, 1969
After watching *Cinderella*, Bobby begins to believe that Carol is a wicked stepmother and that no one cares about him, so he decides to run away.

Brady Tidbits:
Chester Brown is the bully who picks on Bobby.

Episode 11: Vote for Brady
Writer: Elroy Schwartz
Director: David Alexander
Airdate: December 12, 1969
A Brady war erupts, forcing the family to take sides as Marcia and Greg run

against each other for student body president.

Brady Tidbit:
Greg and Marcia attend Fillmore High School.
Alice was a cheerleader.
Cindy beats out Bobby as the new crossing guard for a week.

Brady Pantry:
Alice makes an angel food cake.
Carol makes a salad.

Episode 12: The Voice of Christmas
Writer: John Fenton Murray
Director: Oscar Rudolph
Airdate: December 19, 1969
As Carol is set to sing a Christmas solo, she comes down with laryngitis. While visiting a department store Santa Claus, Cindy tells him that all she wants for Christmas is for her mother's voice to return.

Brady Tidbit:
Alice makes her mother's recipe to cure laryngitis made with mustard power, oil of camford, tar, pepper, vinegar.
Cindy is six years old.
Carol sings "O Come All Ye Faithful."

Episode 13: Is There a Doctor in the House?
Writer: Ruth Brooks Flippen
Director: Oscar Rudolph
Airdate: December 26, 1969

The Brady kids all come down with the measles, leaving Mike and Carol to figure out which one of their personal doctors should become the family doctor.

Brady House Guest:
Marion Ross, "Doctor Potter"
Ross is best known as Marion Cunningham from the '70s hit TV show, *Happy Days*, a role for which she was nominated twice for an Emmy.

Herbert Anderson "Doctor Cameron"
Anderson is best known for his role as Henry Mitchell in *Dennis the Menace*.

Brady Tidbits:
Ms. Kittridge is Greg's algebra teacher.
Mike & Carol sing a parody of "The 12 Days of Christmas."
Mike likes Hot Buttered Rum.

Episode 14: Father of the Year

Writer: Skip Webster
Director: George Cahan
Airdate: January 2, 1970
Marcia submits an essay on Mike for a "Father of the Year" award. While sneaking out of the house to mail the essay, Marcia gets caught and is grounded. After Mike wins the Father of the Year Award, he finds out the real reason for Marcia's behavior.

Brady Tidbits:
Jan quadruple swears.
Cindy tells Carol that Marcia borrowed her perfume.

Brady Motto:
A wise man forgets his anger before he lies down to sleep.

Episode 15: 54–40 and Fight
Writer: Burt Styler
Director: Oscar Rudolph
Airdate: January 9, 1970
The kids fight over what to buy with their "Checker Trading Stamps." In order to decide, the kids build a house of cards. After a mishap, the girls win and they select a color TV so the whole family can enjoy their prize.

Brady Tidbits:
Trading stamps used to be given away at grocery stores, enabling customers to redeem the coupons for merchandise.
The famous moonshine families "Hatfields and McCoys" are mentioned.
The kids get the house of cards ten stories high.

Brady Motto:
It's not if you win or lose, it's how you play the game.

Episode 16: Mike's Horror-Scope
Writer: Ruth Brooks Flippen
Director: David Alexander
Airdate: January 16, 1970
The glamorous and sexy Beebe hires Mike to design her new PINK cosmetic factory. Mike's new female client makes Carol jealous as he begins to neglect his family.

Brady Tidbits:

Martha Sheldon is mentioned as Carol's best friend.

First time it is mentioned that Sam the butcher is Alice's boyfriend.

Brady Pantry:
Carol makes a three-layer cake.

Brady House Guest:
Actress Abbe Lane plays Beebe Gallini and Joe Ross plays the male secretary, Duane Cartwright.

Episode 17: The Undergraduate

Writer: David P. Harmon
Director: Oscar Rudolph
Airdate: January 23, 1970

After Greg flunks a math test, he catches a case of puppy love with Linda, his math teacher.

Brady Tidbit:
Alice mentions that Sam's way of romance is two pounds of heart-shaped liver. Cindy plays with her Kitty Karry-All doll.

Brady Pantry:
Carol is making a chocolate cake.

Brady House Guest:
Wess Parker "Himself"

Parker plays the boyfriend to Greg's math teacher, Miss O'Hara (Gigi Perreau). Parker is best known as a ballplayer for the Los Angeles Dodgers from 1964-1972. He was a six-time "Golden Gloves" winner and a World Series champion in 1965.

Episode 18: Tiger! Tiger!

Writer: Elroy Schwartz
Director: Herb Wallerstein
Airdate: January 30, 1971

After the Bradys' dog Tiger runs away, the family engages in a city-wide search to find him. After offering a reward for his safe return, they find out that Tiger is new father to three puppies.

Brady Pantry:
Alice makes a salad with carrots for dinner.

Episode 19: The Big Sprain

Writer: Tam Spiva
Director: Russ Mayberry
Airdate: February 6, 1970

While Carol is away, Alice sprains her ankle as she is taking care of the household. Mayhem ensues as Mike asks the Brady kids to pitch in and do all the chores themselves.

Sexy-O-Brady:
Alice was going to be Sam's date to the Meat Cutters Ball before hurting her ankle.
Sam and Alice make out under the stars.

Brady Pantry:
Alice makes an apple pie.

Episode 20: Brace Yourself
Writer: Brad Radnitz
Director: Oscar Rudolph
Airdate: February 13, 1970
Marcia gets braces just prior to the big school dance. After her date cancels on her, Marcia fears that everyone thinks she's ugly.

Brady Pantry:
Spaghetti salad and soup is for dinner

Episode 21: The Hero
Writer: Elroy Schwartz
Director: Oscar Rudolph
Airdate: February 20, 1970
Bobby is crowned a hero after he saves a girl in a toy shop. After receiving a lot of attention regarding the incident, it goes directly to Bobby's head.

Brady Pantry:
The Hero's Treat called "Straw-Split-Fudge-Short" includes strawberry shortcake, Hot Fudge Sundae and a Banana Split all on one plate.

Brady Tidbit:
The little girl who Bobby saves is trying to get a Kitty Karry-All doll, just like Cindy's.
Carol's hair goes from being big to being flat throughout the episode – someone contact the wig department, pronto!
In the toy store, the red-headed woman behind Bobby is Barry Williams' stand-in.

Sexy-O-Brady:
Alice is being hit on by Driscoll's delivery man. Then he takes her out to his truck ... now *that's* giving a full delivery.

Episode 22: The Possible Dream
Writer: Al Schwartz & Bill Freedman
Director: Oscar Rudolph
Airdate: February 27, 1970
Cindy discovers Marcia's diary in the garage and mistakenly adds it to their book donation pile. After finding out the status on her diary, Marcia flips out and believes that someone will read about her love for Desi Arnaz, Jr.

Brady Tidbits:
Alice knows the housekeeper for Lucie Arnaz.
Alice has her own diary.
Kitty Karry-All is seen.
The Bradys donate books to the "Friend in Need Society."
Alice in Wonderland is Cindy's favorite story.
Desi Arnaz, Jr. gives Marcia a kiss on the cheek.

Brady Pantry:
Alice is making chocolate chip cookies.

Brady House Guest:
Desi Arnaz, Jr. "Himself"
Arnaz is the son of *I Love Lucy* stars Desi Arnaz and Lucille Ball. In his late teens, Arnaz, Jr. was the drummer for the musical group Dino, Desi, & Billy.

Episode 23: To Move or Not to Move
Writer: Paul West
Director: Oscar Rudolph
Airdate: March 6, 1970

A battle ensues between the kids over the bathroom, making Mike and Carol believe that they need a larger home. The kids don't want to move and turn their home into a haunted house to prevent it from selling.

Brady pantry:
Alice makes cookies.

Episode 24: The Grass is Always Greener
Writer: David P. Harmon
Director: George Cahan
Airdate: March 13, 1970

Mike believes that Carol's girls are easier to watch than his boys. Carol believes that Mike's sons are easier to watch than her girls. After switching kids for the weekend, they each find out the true meaning of "Battle of the Sexes."

Brady Pantry:
Marcia makes dinner: tomato juice, string beans, egg salad, French-fried potatoes, rolls, breaded veal cutlets, and chocolate cake.

Episode 25: Lost Locket, Found Locket
Writer: Charles Hoffman
Director: Norman Abbott
Airdate: March 20, 1970

Jan receives a locket in the mail from an unknown admirer. The Bradys turn into detectives to deduce who sent the locket. It is soon revealed that Alice sent the locket to Jan because she wanted "the middle child" to feel special.

Brady Tidbits:
The Bradys' home address is 422 Clinton Way.
The family's "forgetful" Aunt Martha is mentioned.
Carol's sister's husband is Roger.
Alice is a middle child just like Jan. She has an older sister, Melley, and younger sister, Emily.

Season Two
ABC 1970-1971
Friday 7:30pm

Episode 26: The Dropout
Writer: Ben Gershman & Bill Freedman
Director: Peter Baldwin
Airdate: September 25, 1970
Greg decides to drop out of school after baseball pitcher Don Drysdale drops by the Brady house and encourages him to become a baseball player.

Brady House Guest:
Don Drysdale "Himself"
Drysdale was a pitcher for the Los Angeles Dodgers. He won three world championships. When he retired, his number (#53) was retired from the Dodgers' lineup.

Brady Tidbits:
The opening theme song is now sung by The Brady Kids.

The starting showcases new images of the cast.
Bobby is missing a tooth.
Greg's baseball team is called "Jigers"

Brady Pantry:
Greg's protein milkshake consists of beets, turnips, wheat germ, and cod liver oil.

Episode 27: The Babysitters
Writer: Bruce Howard
Director: Oscar Rudolph
Airdates: October 2, 1970
Mike and Carol have tickets to a sold-out show, leaving Marcia and Greg in charge. However, when Mike and Carol return back home to check up on them, the kids believe that they are prowlers and call the police.

Brady Love:
Alice tries to convince Sam to have her move in with him.

Episode 28: The Slumber Caper
Writer: Tam Spiva
Director: Oscar Rudolph
Airdate: October 9, 1970
Marcia is to have her first slumber party and the boys rebel by playing tricks on the girls. After Marcia is accused of slander toward one of her teachers, the party is in danger of being cancelled.

Brady Tidbits:
Marcia's friends are Jenny Wilton (best friends) and Paula Tardy.

Brady Moto:
Don't blame people until you have all the facts.

Brady Love:
Paula Tardy has a crush on Greg.

Brady Pantry:
Alice makes hot dogs for everyone.

Brady House Guests:
Carolyn Reed "Karen" – Robert Reed's real-life daughter.
Barbara Henderson "Ruthie" – Florence Henderson's real-life daughter.
Hope Sherwood "Jenny" – Sherwood Schwartz's real-life daughter.
Chris Charney (a.k.a. Christine Baranski) "Paula Tardy"
Baranski's stage name as a child was Chris Charney. She is best known for her work in the TV series *Cybill*, where she won an Emmy and was nominated for three more. Most recently she has appeared in *Mama Mia!*, *Chicago* and *The Birdcage*.
E. G. Marshall "Principal J.P. Randolph"
Marshall co-starred with Robert Reed in the TV series *The Defenders*, for which he won two Emmys.

Episode 29: The Un-Underground Movie
Writer: Albert E. Lewin
Director: Jack Arnold
Airdate: October 16, 1970
Greg decides to do a film about the Pilgrims for a school project and the whole family gets involved.

Sexy-O-Brady:
Alice goes cross-dressing in the episode as "John Carver" ..... that's HOT.

Episode 30: Going, Going...Steady
Writer: David P. Harmon
Director: Oscar Rudolph
Airdate: October 23, 1970
Marcia has a hard case of puppy love for Harvey Klinger and learns all she can about bugs to spark his interest in order to go steady.

Brady Tidbit:
Marcia has gone steady with Danny, Alan and Lester.
Marcia is friends with Sally.

Brady Pantry:
Alice serves pot roast for dinner.

Episode 31: Call Me Irresponsible
Writer: Bruce Howard
Director: Hal Cooper
Airdate: October 30, 1970
Greg feels he is old enough to buy a car and he gets hired at Mike's office.

Brady Love:
Greg likes Randy Peterson and wants to take her on a date in his new car.

Episode 32: The Treasures of Sierra Avenue
Writer: Gwen Bagni & Paul Dubov
Director: Oscar Rudolph
Airdate: November 6, 1970

While playing football in an empty lot on Sierra Avenue, Greg, Peter and Bobby find a wallet containing $1,100. The boys return the wallet and receive a $20 reward.

Episode 33: A Fistful of Reasons
Writer: Tam Spiva
Director: Oscar Rudolph
Airdate: November 13, 1970
Kids at school are making fun of Cindy's lisp. As the family works together to help her overcome the issue, Bobby gets a black-eye when he stands up to the school bully in order to protect Cindy.

Brady Pantry:
Alice is whipping up some sweet potatoes

Episode 34: The Not-So-Ugly Duckling
Writer: Paul West
Director: Irving J. Moore
Airdate: November 20, 1970
Jan has a crush on Clark Tyson, but he only has eyes for Marcia. Jan feels that she is an ugly duckling, tries to change her image, and fabricates a boyfriend named George Glass.

Brady Pantry:
Alice is making cinnamon cookies, which are Jan's favorite.

Brady Tidbits:
The Bradys' phone number is 762-0799.
Jan's birthday is in November.
This storyline is used in the movie *The Very Brady Sequel*.

Groovy Note:
The kids' bathroom is missing one of the most important thing – a toilet!!

Episode 35: The Tattle-Tale
Writer: Sam Locke & Milton Pascal
Director: Russ Mayberry
Airdate: December 4, 1970
Cindy is exiled by the other kids for all her tattling. After getting lectured by Mike, Cindy learns her lesson and does not tattle anymore. Not even to help Alice find a registered letter.

Bradywood:
Mike buys the record *The Best of Gilbert & Sullivan*, who are best known for their operas *HMS Pinafore* (1878) and *The Pirates of Penzance* (1879).

Brady Tidbits:
Susan Olsen does not like this particular episode.

Episode 36: What Goes Up...
Writer: William Raynor and Myles Wilder
Director: Leslie H. Martinson
Airdate: December 11, 1970
Bobby climbs up into the tree house, falls and sprains his ankle. The whole ordeal makes him petrified of heights.

Brady Tidbits:
Barry Williams accidentally calls Eve by her real name in this episode instead of her character name of Jan.

Brady Pantry:
Hamburgers are for dinner. Mike and Carol like theirs rare, Peter and Jan like theirs medium rare, and Marcia likes them well done.

Episode 37: Confessions, Confessions
Writer: Brad Radnitz
Director: Russ Mayberry
Airdate: December 18, 1970
While playing basketball in the house, Peter breaks Carol's favorite vase. The kids glue the vase back together so Peter can go on his camping trip. When Carol puts flowers into the vase, water leaks out of it, leading all the kids, except for Peter, to confess that they were the one who broke it.

Brady Tidbit:
This storyline was used in the TV movie *The Brady Bunch in the White House*.

Episode 38: The Impractical Joker
Writer: Burt Styler
Director: Oscar Rudolph
Airdate: January 1, 1971
While pulling a practical joke, Jan loses Greg's mouse that he was using for a project. The joke turns bad when Alice sees the mouse and calls in an exterminator.

Brady Tidbit:
"Myron" is the name of the mouse.
In Barry Williams' book, *Growing Up Brady*, he mentions that this episode is what catapulted Robert Reed's first memo to the producers about the decline of quality scripts.

Episode 39: Where There's Smoke

Writer: David P. Harmon
Director: Oscar Rudolph
Airdate: January 8, 1971

Greg is confronted about his smoking and says that he'll never do it again. When a packet of cigarettes falls out of his letterman's jacket, he becomes determined to find out who they really belong to.

Brady Tidbit:
This is the first episode that Greg sings.
Greg joins a band, The Banana Convention.

Bradywood:
Alice uncovers that the letterman jacket Greg was wearing wasn't really his. Maybe Alice should become one of *Charlie's Angels*.

Episode 40: Will the Real Jan Brady Please Stand Up?

Writer: Al Schwartz and Bill Freedman
Director: Peter Baldwin
Airdate: January 15, 1971

Jan is suffering from being known as the little sister of Marcia. After seeing an ad for wigs, Jan buys one believing that it will help her stand out in a crowd and out of Marcia's shadow.

Brady Tidbits:
Jan gets her wig from the May Company, which was located at the corner of La Brea Blvd & Wilshire Blvd in Los Angeles. Presently, this is the home to the Los Angeles County Museum.

OMB! (Oh My Brady!):
Alice tries on Jan's black wig, making her ready for a drag queen debut!

Brady House Guests:
Pamelyn Ferdin "Lucy Winters"
Ferdin was best known for as being Felix Unger's daughter Enda from *The Odd Couple*.
Marcia Wallace "Saleswoman"
Wallace is best known for her comic timing as Carol Kester Bondurant in *The Bob Newhart Show*.

Episode 41: The Drummer Boy
Writer: Tom and Helen August
Director: Oscar Rudolph
Airdate: January 22, 1971
Peter, Jan and Cindy all get picked to be in the glee club. Disappointed that he didn't make the cut, Bobby decides to learn how to play the drums.

Brady Motto:
Don't pretend to enjoy things just to please others.

OMB!
Peter's football teammates tease him for being in the glee club by calling him a "sissy," "canary," "songbird," and "pom pom girl."

Brady House Guest:
David "Deacon" Jones played for the Los Angeles Rams (1961-1971), San Diego Chargers (1972-1973) and Washington Redskins (1974). In 1980 he was inducted into the Pro Football Hall of Fame.

Episode 42: Coming-Out Party
Writer: David P. Harmon
Director: Oscar Rudolph
Airdate: January 29, 1971

Mike's boss, Mr. Philips, invites the entire family out on his boat for deep-sea diving. When Cindy and Carol need to have their tonsils removed, the boat trip is rescheduled.

Brady Tidbits:
The Ditmiers live next door to the Bradys.

Episode 43: Our Son, the Man
Writer: Albert E. Lewin
Director: Jack Arnold
Airdate: February 5, 1971

Mike's den is turned into a bedroom for Greg after he complains about his lack of privacy in sharing a room with Bobby and Peter.

Brady Tidbit:
Greg wears a "West Dale High School" shirt.

Episode 44: The Liberation of Marcia Brady
Writer: Charles Hoffman
Director: Russ Mayberry
Airdate: February 12, 1971

The Battle of the Sexes begins once again as Marcia feels that girls can do anything boys can. Marcia joins the Frontier Scouts, leading Peter to join the Sunflower Girls. In the end, Marcia proves that she was right.

Sexy-O-Brady:
Peter is one PRETTY HOT Sunflower Girl selling his cookies!

Episode 45: Lights Out
Writer: Bruce Howard
Director: Oscar Rudolph
Airdate: February 19, 1971
After seeing a magician perform, Cindy is afraid of sleeping in the dark. Peter takes up tricks on his own as "Peter the Great" and has Cindy become his assistant in order to help her conquer her fear.

Brady Tidbits:
In Barry Williams' book, *Growing Up Brady*, he mentions that the judges are Florence and Barry's real stand-ins.

Episode 46: The Winner
Writer: Elroy Schwartz
Director: Robert Reed
Airdate: February 26, 1971
When Cindy wins an award, Bobby feels left out since he has never won a trophy of his own. In order to prove himself, he enters an ice cream contest.

Brady Pantry:
Spaghetti is for dinner.

Brady Tidbit:
Robert Reed directs this episode, the first of four.
Mike, Carol and Bobby leave for the contest in a blue convertible and come back in the Brady station wagon.

Episode 47: Double Parked

Writer: Skip Webster
Director: Jack Arnold
Airdate: March 5, 1971
Mike's job is jeopardized when Carol and kids ban together to save Wood Park, the location that Mike's firm is set to erect a new office building.

Brady Pantry:
Alice makes chicken for dinner.

Sexy-O-Brady:
Alice uses her sexuality to have a man sign the park petition. Talk about steamy...and she wasn't asking to see his side of beef.

Episode 48: Alice's September Song

Writer: Elroy Schwartz
Director: Oscar Rudolph
Airdate: March 12, 1971
Alice's old boyfriend, Mark Mallard, arrives and sweeps her off her feet. However, he only wants to scam Alice out of her money in order to float his gambling habit.

Episode 49: Tell It Like It Is

Writer: Charles Hoffman
Director: Terry Becker
Airdate: March 26, 1971
Carol is writing a story about the family for *Tomorrow's Woman* magazine. When the story is rejected for not being "rosy" enough, she does a rewrite.

Sexy-O-Brady:
Alice dreamed about being crowned Ms. America. Move over Sandra Bullock, Alice is on her way for the third installment of *Miss Congeniality: Pork Chops & Applesauce*.

Season 3
ABC; 1971-1972
Friday 8:00pm

Episode #50: Ghost Town USA (part 1 of 3)
Airdate: September 17, 1971
Writer: Tam Spiva
Director: Oscar Rudolph
Mike and Carol surprise the kids and Alice with a camping vacation to the Grand Canyon. They discover there is a ghost town nearby and spend the night there. After settling in, a stranger shows up who thinks that the Bradys are there to steal his gold. He locks them in the jailhouse and steals their car. Mike pulls some *MacGyver* maneuvers to get the keys off the wall. After escaping from the jail, Mike and Peter begin the 20-mile walk back to the main road to get help as the others stay back and pray for water and food.

Brady Tidbit:
The ghost town used in this episode was filmed on the *Bonanza* set. During their downtime from filming, the Brady boys would pretend to be cowboys, and reenact gun fights.

Brady House Guest:
Jim Backus "Zaccariah T. Brown"
Backus plays the man who thinks the Bradys want to steal his gold. He was best known for his work as Thurston Howell, III on Sherwood's other hit

series, *Gilligan's Island*. He was also the iconic voice of the cartoon character Mr. Magoo.

Brady Pantry:
Alice cooks chicken on the grill that looks just like KFC original flavor.

Sexy-O-Brady:
Cindy and Jan pretend to be saloon girls of the Old West. Now, that is so perfectly wholesome Brady!

Episode #51: Grand Canyon or Bust (Part 2 of 3)
Airdate: September 24, 1971
Writer: Tam Spiva
Director: Oscar Rudolph
Mike and Peter eventually return with their car and continue on their vacation to the Grand Canyon. Upon arriving, the group travel down into the Canyon on mules to set up camp on the basin. Cindy and Bobby end up wandering off, forcing the rest of the clan to do an all-out search to find them.

OMB!:
Alice acts like a real "ass." When the mule will not pull the plow, they made Alice do it instead!

Episode #52: The Brady Braves (Part 3 of 3)
Airdate: October 1. 1971
Writer: Tam Spiva
Director: Oscar Rudolph
A young Indian boy helps Cindy and Bobby find their way back to camp. They venture out again to bring food to their new friend. Eventually, Mike

finds them and gives the young boy some fatherly advice. Upon returning back home, the boy's grandfather is so grateful, that he throws a party for the Bradys and inducts them into their Indian tribe.

Brady Pantry:
Alice cooks hot dogs and beans! Bobby puts some beans in his flashlight and pockets several hot dogs for their runaway Indian friend.

Brady Motto:
You can give someone the best advice, but you can't make them accept it.

Brady Indian Names:
Mike	Big Eagle of Large Nest
Carol	Yellow Flower with Many Peddles
Greg	Stalking Wolf
Peter	Middle Buffalo or Sleeping Lizard
Cindy	Wondering Blossom
Bobby	Little Bear Who Loses Way
Jan	Dove of Morning Light
Marcia	Willow Dancing in Wind
Alice	Swallow in Waiting

Episode #53: The Wheeler-Dealer
Writer: Bill Freedman and Ben Gershman
Director: Jack Arnold
Airdate: October 8. 1971
Greg gets his drivers' license and buys a beat up car for only $100. Greg tries to do all the repairs himself and finds nothing can make his "lemon" run.

Bradywood:
Mike reminds Greg that they are not the Onassises. Aristotle Onassis, a wealthy aristocrat, was once married to American royalty, Jacqueline Kennedy.

Brady Tidbit:
The opening theme song is re-recorded again by The Brady Kids.
The starting showcases new images of the cast.
Car Sports magazine was seen in two other episodes in season 2.

Episode #54: My Sister, Benedict Arnold
Writer: Elroy Schwartz
Director: Hal Cooper
Airdate: October 15. 1971
Marcia and Greg begin fighting after Marcia starts dating his rival, Warren Mulaney. Out of spite, Marcia continues to date Warren, forcing Greg to start dating Marcia's rival, Kathy Lawrence.

Episode #55: The Personality Kid
Writer: Ben Starr
Director: Oscar Rudolph
Airdate: October 22. 1971
Peter believes he has no personality and the entire family tries to help build his self-esteem. As Peter begins to imitate other people to become more interesting, he finds out that being himself is the best personality of all.

Brady Tidbit:
Peter recites those famous words, "Pork Chops & Applesauce."
Kathy Lawrence (Sheri Cowart) is now Marcia's friend, yet in the episode "My Sister, Benedict Arnold," they were rivals.

Sexy-O-Brady:
Greg looks like a grape dressed all in purple! His shirt matches his purple pants – now that is ultra-styling.

Episode #56: Juliet is the Sun
Writer: Brad Radnitz
Director: Jack Arnold
Airdate: October 29. 1971
Marcia, Peter and Jan are all cast in the play *Romeo & Juliet*. When Marcia gets the lead, she wants to back out due to lack of confidence. As the family joins together to build up her ego, they create a diva!

Brady Tidbit:
Marcia mentions that she needs to brush her hair 100 times, three times a day, in order to keep it so beautiful.

OMB!:
Greg is wearing the same purple outfit that he wore in "The Personality Kid!" Shame, shame, shame on you, Greg, you can't wear the same thing twice. He doesn't stop there, as he continues to wear the same outfit throughout rest of the season.

Episode #57: Now a Word from our Sponsor
Writer: Albert E. Lewin
Director: Peter Baldwin
Airdate: November 5, 1971
The Bradys are chosen for a 'Safe' laundry soap TV commercial. After they ask an actress to help with their thespian skills, they lose the commercial due to overacting.

Brady Tidbit:
Bobby uses "Safe" laundry soap in the episode ("Law & Disorder," #86) where he uses too much soap, causing the washing machine to overflow with suds

Episode #58: The Private Ear
Writer: Michael Morris
Director: Hal Cooper
Airdate: November 12, 1971
Peter is secretly recording the family in order to find out all their personal secrets. In passing, Peter reveals all the secrets causing a fight to ensue between the siblings.

OMB!:
For the third time Greg is wearing his purple outfit.

Episode #59 Her Sister's Shadow
Teleplay: Al Schwartz and Phil Leslie
Story by: Al Schwartz and Ray Singer
Director: Russ Mayberry
Airdate: November 19, 1971
Once again, Jan feels that she is always in Marcia's shadow. In order to prove herself, she decides to try out to be a Pom Pom girl.

Brady Tidbit:
Jan recites her infamous saying, "Marcia, Marcia, Marcia" and she starts hearing voices in her head!!!!

Bradywood:
Greg does a pom pom cheer! I bet the Dallas Cowboys cheerleading team would love to have him.

Brady Moto:
Find what you're good at and do your best at it.

Episode #60 Click
Written: Tom and Helen August
Director: Oscar Rudolph
Airdate: November 26, 1971
Greg makes the football team, but is eliminated after he fractures his rib. While on the sidelines, he takes a photo that helps his team win the game and becomes the team's official photographer.

Sexy-O-Brady:
Greg shows off his abs under his football uniform. Who knew that any of the Bradys had abs?

Brady Pantry:
Alice's sandwiches are in high demand as Cindy uses one to trade for a turtle.

Episode #61 Getting Davy Jones
Written: Phil Leslie and Al Schwartz
Director: Oscar Rudolph
Airdate: December 10, 1971
Marcia says that she can get Davy Jones to entertain at their school prom since she is the president of his fan club. As the word spreads like wildfire, she is unable to get in touch with him.

134 The Brady Bunch

Brady House Guest:
Davy Jones "Himself"
Teenage heartthrob Jones sings his hit song, "Girl." Jones was best known for being a part of the TV band The Monkees. Jones reprised his role in *The Brady Bunch Movie* and sang the exact same song.
Marcia Wallace "Ms. Robbins"
In her second appearance, Wallace plays Marcia's teacher. She was last seen in "Will the Real Jan Brady Please Stand Up?" (#40).

OMB!:
Marcia and Greg pretend to be bus boys in order to meet Davy Jones. As Marcia throws an air kiss to Greg, Davy Jones' manager thinks of only one thing ... gay, gay, gay.

Episode #62: The Not-So-Rose-Colored Glasses
Written: Bruce Howard
Director: Leslie H. Martinson
Airdate: December 24, 1971
Jan becomes very self-conscious when she has to get glasses. Not wanting to wear them, Jan takes off the glasses and runs her bike into a group photograph of the kids that was going to be Mike's anniversary present for Carol.

OMB!:
The flamboyant photographer is named Gregory Gaylord (Robert Nadder). His character's name describes the character perfectly.

Episode #63: The Teeter-Totter Caper
Written: Joel Kane and Jack Lloyd
Director: Russ Mayberry
Airdate: December 31, 1971
Cindy and Bobby feel they are too small to help out with anything. In order to prove themselves, they decided to make a new teeter-totter record.

Brady Tidbit:
Cousin Gertrude is getting married.
The kids like to watch the TV show *Kartoon King*.

Episode #64: Big Little Man
Written: Skip Webster
Director: Robert Reed
Airdate: January 7, 1972
When Greg saves him from almost falling off the side of the house, Bobby feels that being so little is the worst thing possible. After getting locked in Sam's meat locker, Greg breaks the window in the door, in which Bobby is able to crawl through and save them both.

Brady Tidbit:
Robert Reed's second time in the director's chair.
Fresh beef tongue is only fifty-five cents.
Bobby's favorite dessert is strawberry shortcake.
This storyline of this episode is very similar to "My Brother's Keeper" (#103)

Episode #65: Dough Re Mi

Written: Ben Starr
Director: Allen Baron
Airdate: January 14, 1972

Greg becomes a songwriter and creates the "Brady Six" singing group. Right before they go into the studio to record the song, Peter's voice begins to change, so Greg writes a song to reflect this.

Brady Pantry:
Alice grills hamburgers.

Brady Tidbit:
This marks the beginning of the Brady Kids as singing sensations.
The two songs the Brady kids sing, "Time to Change" and "We Can Make the World a Whole Lot Brighter," were released on the record *Meet the Brady Bunch* in 1972. They were later released on the CD *It's a Sunshine Day: The Best of The Brady Bunch*.
Allen Baron was also a director for *Charlie's Angels*.

Episode #66: Jan's Aunt Jenny

Written: Michael Morris
Director: Hal Cooper
Airdate: January 21, 1972

Jan finds out that she has a striking resemblance to her Aunt Jenny when she was young. After asking her aunt for a recent photo, Jan is scared to death that she'll look just like her when she grows up. When Aunt Jenny arrives, Jan realizes that personality matters more than how a person looks.

Brady House Guest:
Imogene Coca "Aunt Jenny"
Comedienne Coca is best known for appearing on *Your Show of Shows* opposite Sid Caesar. She was nominated for a Tony, won an Emmy in 1952 and was nominated for five others. She will always be remembered as Aunt Edna in *National Lampoon's Vacation* who dies on the trip.

Episode #67: The Big Bet
Written: Elroy Schwartz
Director: Earl Bellamy
Airdate: January 28, 1972
When Greg believes he can do double the amount of the chin-ups that Bobby can do, Bobby puts Greg to the challenge. Upon losing, Greg has to do a week's worth of chores for Bobby.

Brady House Guest:
Hope Sherwood "Rachel"
Sherwood's second appearance on the show and the first time as Greg's girlfriend.

Episode #68: The Power of the Press
Written: Ben Gershman and Bill Freedman
Director: Jack Arnold
Airdate: February 4, 1972
Peter is the new reporter for the school newspaper. As he becomes the hit of the school, Peter's school work begins to suffer.

Brady Tidbit:
"Scoop Brady" is Peter's writing name.

Brady Motto:
Learning honesty is the best policy.

Sexy-O-Brady:
Mike was cutting edge wearing a "Hang-Ten" t-shirt.

Episode #69: Sergeant Emma
Written: Harry Winkler
Director: Jack Arnold
Airdate: February 11, 1972
While Alice is on vacation, her cousin Emma comes to help out the family. Emma's Army background whips the Bradys into military shape.

Brady Tidbit:
Cousin Emma was played by Ann B. Davis.

Brady Pantry:
Beef Eisenhower, Succotash Pentagon, and Potatoes MacArthur

Sexy-O-Brady:
Emma is a very masculine-like sergeant who keeps everyone in line ... girls, it's time to hit the showers. Who wants to drop the soap first?

Episode #70: Cindy Brady, Lady
Written: Al Schwartz and Larry Rhine
Director: Hal Cooper
Airdate: February 18, 1972
Tired of being young, Cindy wants to become older like her sisters. Bobby plays her secret admirer to help her feel special.

Brady Tidbit:
This marks Cindy's first date with Tommy Jamison (Eric Shea)

Episode #71: My Fair Opponent
Written: Bernie Kahn
Director: Peter Baldwin
Airdate: March 3, 1972
As a senior prank, a homely girl is nominated for banquet hostess. Upset over this, Marcia takes the girl under her wing, gives her a make-over, and makes her popular.

Bradywood:
This is the Brady version of *My Fair Lady*; Marcia plays a Professor Henry Higgins-like character who transforms the homely girl into a pretty one.

Episode #72: The Fender Bender
Written: David P. Harmon
Director: Alan Baron
Airdate: March 10, 1972
Carol has a fender bender in a grocery store parking lot. After being taken to court by the man who hit her, the court rules in Carol's favor.

Brady Pantry:
Chicken and Dumplings are served for dinner.

Season Four
ABC; 1972-1973
Friday 8:00pm

Episode #73: Hawaiian Bound
Written: Tam Spiva
Director: Jack Arnold
Airdate: September 22, 1972
Mike has to check on the construction of a building he designed and takes the entire family to Hawaii. Bobby finds a Tabu idol, which brings bad luck and is passed around the family.

Brady House Guest:
Don Ho "Himself"
Ho plays himself when he meets Bobby and Cindy and sings them a song. Ho was best known for his song "Tiny Bubbles" and was an island native.

Brady Tidbit:
The family flies United Airlines and stays at the Sheraton Waikiki
Kipula Construction Co. is building Mike's building
Robert, Barry and Christopher's hair goes curly due to the humid Hawaiian weather.

Sexy-O-Brady:
Alice gets lei'ed (a necklace of flowers) by the Hawaiian welcome girls over and over again! Also, Mike and Greg are found shirtless ... yummy Brady boys.

Chapter Seven 141

groovy tip!

In 1996, the alternative band The Presidents of the United States of America released the song "Tiki God" on their *II* album. The group sings about how Bobby found the Tiki god in the Hawaiian episodes.

The Brady Family Test

Here is a quick test to see if you're a Brady. If you answer yes to all these ...well, time to get back to your house on Clinton Way!

1. Is your sliding glass door missing the glass in it?
2. Has your dog been missing for years, but you keep the doghouse anyway in the backyard?
3. Does your housekeeper date the butcher for good prices on meat?
4. Do you have Astroturf for grass?
5. Do you hear voices as just part of your day?
6. Do you have a payphone in the house?
7. Do you find yourself singing (or replaced) on a short-lived variety show?
8. Do you find that your home does not have a toilet in the bathroom?
9. Do find yourself wearing a black wig on good days?
10. Do you have a Tabu idol that brings you good luck?

Episode #74: Pass the Tabu

Written: Tam Spiva
Director: Jack Arnold
Airdate: September 29, 1972

Jan finds the Tabu statue and a spider crawls into her bag and finds his way into Peter's bed. The boys uncover the story behind the Tabu and venture to the burial ground to return the statue and reverse the curse.

Episode #75: The Tiki Caves

Written: Tam Spiva
Director: Jack Arnold
Airdate: October 6, 1972

While the boys return the Tabu statue, Professor Whitehead kidnaps them after he thinks they want to steal his archaeology find. Mike and Carol rescue them from the crazy Professor.

Brady House Guests:

Vincent Price "Professor Hubert Whitehead"
Price plays Professor Whitehead who kidnaps the boys. Price was best known as the king of horror films and did the opening rap for Michael Jackson's song "Thriller." He was also a guest on *The Brady Bunch Variety Hour*.

Sexy-O-Brady:

The Professor ties the boys up. Brady bondage is fun.

Episode #76: Today, I am a Freshman

Written: William Raynor and Miles Wilder
Director: Hal Cooper
Airdate: October 13, 1972

Marcia is frightened about entering high school with all her friends going to another school. She quickly joins all the school clubs only to find out she should just be herself to make friends.

Brady Tidbit:
This is the episode Peter makes the volcano which explodes on Marsha and her friends.

Episode #77: Cyrano De Brady
Written: Skip Weber
Director: Hal Cooperf
Airdate: October 20, 1972
Peter falls for a girl, but is all left feet when she is around. Greg tries to help Peter woo her, but she then falls for Greg.

Bradywood:
Peter uses the classic 1897 play *Cyrano de Bergerac* by Edmond Rostand to get his girl.

Episode #78: Fright Night (Halloween Episode)
Written: Brad Radnitz
Director: Jerry London
Airdate: October 27, 1972
The girls see a ghost which turns out to be a trick by their brothers. The girls get back on the boys by haunting the attic but when all the kids want to frighten Alice, Carol's third-place sculpture is broken.

Bradywood:
The Brady girls become detectives to uncover their ghost. They might be young, but they sure are *Charlie's Angels* in training.

Episode #79: The Show Must Go On?
Written: Harry Winkler
Director: Jack Donohue
Airdate: November 3, 1972
Carol and Marcia are to sing a mother/daughter duet as Mike and Greg read a poem at the Westdale H.S. Family Night Frolics.

Brady Tidbit:
Frank DeVol, who co-wrote the Brady opening music, is the baldheaded man playing the musical instrument at the Frolics.

Bradywood:
Carol and Marcia sing 'Together (Wherever We Go)" from the Stephen Sondheim-Jule Styne's Broadway show *Gypsy*.

Episode #80: Jan, The Only Child
Written: Al Schwartz and Ralph Goodman
Director: Roger Duchowny
Airdate: November 11, 1972
Jan seems to be overlooked and wishes she didn't have to do family things - she wants to be an only child. When Jan makes a deal with the kids that they are invisible, she begins to understand how much she loves her brothers and sisters.

OMB!:
The Bradys are a full square at the square dance. Now these good down-home Bradys sure could be contestants on *Dancing with the Stars*.

Brady Tidbit:
This is the episode were the whole family does the potato sack race.

Episode #81: Career Fever
Written: Burt and Adele Styler
Director: Jerry London
Airdate: November 17, 1972
Mike thinks Greg wants to be an architect. Instead of telling Mike that he doesn't want to be an architect, Greg digs himself deeper into the lie.

Episode #82: Goodbye, Alice, Hello
Written: Milton Rosen
Director: George Tyne
Airdate: November 24, 1972
When the kids feel they can't trust Alice anymore, Alice asks her friend to fill for her until she decides if she will stay with the Bradys. The kids miss Alice and they all go and bring her back.

Episode #83: Greg's Triangle
Written: Bill Freedman and Ben Gershman
Director: Richard Michaels
Airdate: December 8, 1972
Greg falls for Jennifer Nichols, who is using his affections to win his vote to become head cheerleader.

Sexy-O-Brady:
A sexy, hot, bare-chested Greg Brady is seen on the beach in a bathing suit. GRRRRRR.

Brady House Guest:
Rita Wilson "Pat Conway"
Wilson plays a cheerleader contestant. Wilson appeared in numerous

films, such as *Sleepless in Seattle*, and produced the hit films as *Mama Mia!* and *My Fat Greek Wedding*. She is married actor Tom Hanks. This was her very first role as an actress.

Episode #84: Everyone Can't Be George Washington

Written: Sam Locke and Milton Pascal
Director: Richard Michaels
Airdate: December 22, 1972

Peter is auditioning for the role of George Washington, but is crushed when he gets the role of Benedict Arnold instead. When the school kids boo and hiss him for playing a traitor, he tries hard to get out of playing the role. But when he is out of the play, the whole play is canceled.

Brady House Guest:

Barbara Bernstein "Peggy"

This is Bernstein's, the daughter of Florence Henderson, second appearance on the show.

You know your having a Jan Day when....

1. When you start saying: Marcia, Marcia, Marcia
2. When your wig is all wrong
3. When you have to get glasses to see
4. When your made-up boyfriend dumps you
5. When you find a big spider in your purse
6. When you're invisible to everyone around you
7. When everyone is acting invisible to *you*.
8. When you start hearing voices.
9. When the boy you like falls for someone else, like Marcia.
10. When you screw up an engraving order.

Episode #85: Love and the Older Man

Written: Martin A. Ragaway
Director: George Tyne
Airdate: January 5, 1973
Marcia falls head over heels for the new dentist.

Brady Tidbit:

Jan reads *Teentime Romance* magazines

Brady Pantry:

Alice makes meatloaf for dinner.

Episode #86: Law & Disorder

Written: Elroy Schwartz
Director: Hal Cooper
Airdate: January 12, 1973

Bobby is named the "Safety Monitor" and his whole class hates him when the responsibility goes to his head. Bobby finds that rules are made to be broken sometimes when he rescues a cat.

Brady Tidbit:
The Brady boat is named the S.S. *Brady*.
This is the episode where the washing machine overflows with suds.
The word "stinker" is used again in this episode.

Sexy-O-Brady:
Bobby splits his pants ... now that is one breezy Brady crack.

Episode #87: Greg Gets Grounded

Written: Elroy Schwartz
Director: Jack Arnold
Airdate: January 19, 1973

Greg is grounded from driving the family car. After he borrows a neighbor's car to pick up his rock show tickets, he is grounded again. He makes a deal that he live by his exact words, which gets him into trouble.

Brady Tidbit:
Bobby buys a toad named "Spunker" and "Old Grogger."
The same movie is playing in the drive-in as the last time they were at the theater.

Brady House Guest:
Hope Sherwood "Rachel"
Sherwood guest stars a third time in the series. Hope went on to write future Brady adventures as *A Very Brady Musical* (2008) with her brother Lloyd Schwartz.

Episode #88: Amateur Night
Written: Sam Locke and Milton Pascal
Director: Jack Arnold
Airdate: January 26, 1973

Jan orders engraving on the sliver platter for their parents' anniversary, which the kids can't afford. The kids enter the *Pete Sterne Amateur Hour* as "The Silver Platters" to win the money. Unfortunately, the kids come in third place.

Brady Tidbit:
The songs, "It's a Sunshine Day" and "Keep On," the kids sing in the show were originally released on the 1972 album *Kids from the Brady Bunch*. Today, the songs are available on *It's a Sunshine Day: The Best of The Brady Bunch* CD. The songs the kids sing were also heard in *The Brady Bunch Movie*.

KBEX-TV is a fictional TV station and was used in many TV shows such as *Charlie's Angels, Mission: Impossible, What's Happening!!* and *MacGyver*.

Episode #89: Bobby's Hero
Written: Michael Morris
Director: Leslie H. Martinson
Airdate: February 2, 1973

Bobby's hero is outlaw Jesse James. Carol and Mike want Bobby to understand that Jesse James was no American hero, which he realizes after he meets a man whose father was killed by James.

Brady Tidbit:
This is the episode Bobby dreams James kills the Brady family.

Brady Pantry:
Pepperoni pizza and salad for dinner

Episode #90: The Subject Was Noses
Written: Al Schwartz and Larry Rhine
Director: Jack Arnold
Airdate: February 9, 1973
Marcia is hit in the face by a football. Doug, the high-school football star, cancels their date. When her noise is back to normal, Doug changes his mind about the date, but Marcia decides to go with Charlie.

Brady Tidbit:
This is the Brady classic episode where Marcia is hit in the nose with a football. This was recreated for *The Brady Bunch Movie*.

Episode #91: How to Succeed In Business
Written: Gene Thompson
Director: Robert Reed
Airdate: February 23, 1973
Peter gets his first job at the bike shop. He works too hard on only one bike and is fired, but decides not to tell the family right away.

Brady Tidbit:
This is the third episode Robert Reed directed.

Episode #92: The Great Earring Caper
Written: Larry Rhine and Al Schwartz
Director: Leslie H. Martinson
Airdate: March 2, 1973
Cindy was trying on Mom's earnings and then they disappear. Peter uses his detective skills to find out what happened with them.

Sexy-O-Brady:
Mike Brady has a great pair of legs when dressed up as Mark Antony

Episode #93 You're Never Too Old
Written: Ben Gershman and Bill Freedman
Director: Bruce Bilson
Airdate: March 9, 1973
Marcia and Jan play matchmaker with Grandma Hutchins and Grandpa Brady, which turns into true love and they fly off to Las Vegas to get married.

Brady House Guest:
Florence Henderson plays Grandma Connie Hutchins and Robert Reed is Grandpa Judge Henry "Hank."

Episode #94: You Can't Win 'em All
Written: Lois Hire
Director: Jack Donohue
Airdate: March 16, 1973
Cindy and Bobby are picked to take the test to be on the TV show *Question the Kids*. Cindy is picked and gets a really big head about being a television star, but then freezes up on the air.

Episode #95: A Room at the Top
Written: William Raynor and Myles Wilder
Director: Lloyd Schwartz
Airdate: March 23, 1973
Marcia and Greg are both promised the attic for their room. Greg is given the room, but gives the room up for Marcia. Marcia then gives it back to Greg.

OMB!:
The attic storyline is used in *A Very Brady Sequel*, as both Greg and Marcia share the attic and their flames of passion for each other begin to spark. Oh Greg ... Oh Marcia ...

Chapter Seven 153

The beautiful Mrs. Brady: the wonderful ... Ms. Florence Henderson!
(image courtesy of Ms. Henderson)

Mike Brady's Some Famous mottos

- Sometime when we lose we win.
- Bradys don't go back on their promise.
- You can't take a step forward with both feet still on the ground.
- A wise man forgets his anger before he lies down to sleep.
- Money and fame are very important things, but there are things more important, like people.
- Find out what you can do best and then do your best with it.

Season Five
ABC; 1973-1974
Friday 8:00pm

Episode #96: Adios, Johnny Bravo
Written: Joanna Lee
Director: Jerry London
Airdate: September 14, 1973
The Brady kids have booked a singing gig on *Hal Baron Talent Show* and Greg is discovered by an agent. They want Greg to be the new music sensation "Johnny Bravo," but Carol and Mike want him to attend college.

Brady Tidbit:
New hairstyles: Carol has a new short bob and Cindy now has braided pigtails.

Three songs were sung on this opening-season episode, "You've Got to Be in Love (to Love a Love Song)," "Good Time Music," "Heading to the Mountains." They were never released onto any of their records.

Barry Williams released the 1999 CD, *The Return of Johnny Bravo*, which was to celebrate the 30th Anniversary of *The Brady Bunch*. The album included a new song, "Johnny's Back."

Brady House Guest:
Claudia Jennings "Tammy Cutler"
Jennings plays the agent who wants to represent Greg. Jennings was an up-and-coming actress and a *Playboy* Playmate. In 1979, she auditioned for the role of Tiffany Wells in *Charlie's Angels*, but did not win the job. She was killed in a car accident in 1979.

Sexy-O-Brady:
Greg gets mulled by a group of girls and has his shirt ripped to shreds … good, girls, now go for the pants!

Episode #97: Mail Order Hero
Written: Martin Ragaway
Director: Bruce Bilson
Airdate: September 21, 1973
Bobby dreams of playing football with Joe Namath. After Bobby tells a white lie about knowing Namath to his friends, they all can't wait to meet him. Cindy sends a letter to Namath that Bobby is sick and he pays a visit.

Brady Tidbit:
Football numbers: Bobby (#84) and Joe (#12).
Bradys' phone number 555-6161

Brady Pantry:
Alice makes brownies

Brady House Guests:
Joe Namath "Himself"
Namath plays himself in this episode. He played for the Jets from 1965-1976, and then moved to the Los Angeles Rams in 1977. He won the Super Bowl in 1969 and his New York Jets number #12 was retired and he was inducted into the Hall of Fame.

Episode #98: Snow White and the Seven Bradys
Written: Ben Starr
Director: Bruce Bilson
Airdate: September 28, 1973
Cindy wants to raise $200 for a set of rare books for a retiring teacher and she offers her family to perform *Snow White and the Seven Dwarfs*. When there is a mistake with the theater, they perform the play in the Bradys' backyard.

Sexy-O-Brady:
The Brady version of *Snow White* is super-groovy, with Alice as the evil queen dressed in a purple outfit, making all the drag queens jealous.

Episode #99: Never Too Young
Written: Al Schwartz and Larry Rhine
Director: Richard Michaels
Airdate: October 5, 1973
Bobby sees fireworks after his first kiss from Millicent and Cindy is a witness. Bobby might have contracted the mumps from her kiss and stays way from the family so not to infect them.

Brady Tidbit:
Bobby was the only Brady to have an on-camera kiss during the five-year run.
Carol and Mike sing "I Wanna Be Loved by You."

Sexy-O-Brady:
When Bobby and Millicent do a slow run, twirl and then a kiss … oh my goodness, isn't that super-sweet?

Brady House Guest:
Melissa Anderson "Millicent"
Anderson is the little girl who gives Bobby his first kiss. Anderson went on to play Mary Ingalls in the hit series *Little House on the Prairie*, for which she was nominated for an Emmy. She won an Emmy in 1980 for her role in the *Afterschool Special*, "Which Mother is Mine?"

Episode #100: Peter the Wolf

Written: Tam Spiva
Director: Leslie H. Martinson
Airdate: October 12, 1973
Greg has a hot date and asks Peter to double date. When the girls uncover Greg's lie about Peter's age, they play a trick on them which backfires with Mike possibly losing a client.

Brady Tidbit:
The movie playing was the same the last two times Greg took dates to the drive-in.

Bradywood:
When Peter loses his mustache.

Episode #101: Getting Greg's Goat

Written: Milton Pascal and Sam Locke
Director: Robert Reed
Airdate: October 19, 1973

Greg kidnaps the Coolidge High School team mascot goat as a school prank. The kids think Greg is keeping a girl upstairs in his room.

Brady Pantry:
Alice makes flapjacks for breakfast.

Brady Tidbit:
This is the fourth and final episode that Robert Reed directed.

Brady House Guest:
Sandra Gould "Mrs. Gould"
She was on the committee to punish the one who stole the mascots. Gould is best known for her work as the nosy neighbor Gladys Kravitz on *Bewitched*.

Episode #102: Marcia Gets Creamed

Written: Ben Gershman & Bill Freedman
Director: Peter Baldwin
Airdate: October 26, 1973

Marcia gets a job at the ice cream shop. She hires Peter, yet fires him because he's lazy and then she hires Jan. When the owner comes back, he chooses to keep Jan and fires Marcia.

Sexy-O-Brady:
Bobby is spit-shining shoes...HUMMMM.....gotta start your fetishes early!

Brady Pantry:
Pot roast for dinner

Brady Motto:
Business before pleasure

Episode #103: My Brother's Keeper
Written: Michael Morris
Director: Ross Bowman
Airdate: November 2, 1973
Bobby saves Peter's life after pushing him out of the way of a falling ladder. Peter becomes Bobby's slave until Peter saves Bobby when he locked in the closet.

Brady Tidbit:
This episode is very similar to "Big Little Man" (#64).
Only time the tub is used in the bathroom.
The reason the Bradys did not have a toilet was because of the FCC (Federal Communications Commission) rule at the time that TV shows could not show a toilet on camera.

Sexy-O-Brady:
Bobby goes to the bathroom and flushes the toilet. (we hear the flush off camera) How can this be?? – The Bradys' don't have a toilet in the bathroom!!

Brady Pantry:
Alice makes Hungarian Goulash.

Episode #104: Quarterback Sneak
Written: Ben Gershman & Bill Freedman
Director: Peter Baldwin
Airdate: November 9, 1973
Marcia falls for the head of a rival football team who uses her to steal the Westdale playbook.

The Romance of Sam

Sam always was giving Alice a freebee when he delivered his meat. Here are some ideas what he was looking for with each meat he gave!

Side of Beef – a real groovy lay.
Lamb – a sweet date.
Rump Roast – going right for some raunchy sex in the bedroom.
Chicken - scared to ask "the" question.
Deli Slices – smooth talking her into anything.
Ham – one way he makes her giggle.
Sirloin Steaks – for those special occasions.
Liver – it's just true love

Episode #105: Try, Try Again
Written: Al Schwartz & Larry Rhine
Director: George Tyne
Airdate: November 16, 1973
Jan quits ballet after she does not make the recital and loses her self-confidence. She tries tap and acting, but finds out she is great as a painter.

Brady Tidbit:
Eve Plum is a true artist with her very own paintings, which one can buy on her official website: www.eveplum.tv.

Bradywood:
Peter and Bobby call themselves Elizabeth Taylor and Richard Burton, the famous acting couple … but even better, Alice thinks she has tons in common with screen legends Raquel Welch and Shirley Temple.

Episode #106: The Cincinnati Kids
Written: Al Schwartz & Larry Rhine
Director: Leslie H. Martinson
Airdate: November 23, 1973
Mike is working on an amusement park in Cincinnati and brings along the whole family. While in the park, his plans go missing. Jan finds the plans and the family relays them across the park.

Brady Tidbit:
Kings Island Amusement Park was used in this episode and is located around Cincinnati, Ohio.

Brady House Guest:
Lloyd L. Schwartz "Bear"
Producer and son of Schwartz guest stars as a guy who is wearing a bear outfit.
Hilary Thompson 'Marge'
Thompson plays the girl Greg falls for. She plays "Sabrina Duncan" in an episode of *Charlie's Angels* called "Counterfeit Angels."

Episode #107: The Elopement

Written: Harry Winkler
Director: Jerry London
Airdate: December 7, 1973
The kids think Alice and Sam are going to elope. The family plans to throw a wedding reception. But when Alice & Sam have a fight, the family tries get them back together.

Brady Tidbit:
At the end of this episode, Alice says she and Sam are engaged. But in the following episodes, she still is hoping he will ask her.

Brady Pantry:
Alice makes a full turkey for dinner.

Sexy-O-Brady:
Sam's bowing team is "Meat Packers" – now *that* name says it all.

Episode #108: Miss Popularity

Written: Martin Ragaway
Director: Jack Donohue
Airdate: December 21, 1973
Jan is nominated for "Most Popular Girl" in school. The entire family pitches in to help her, but when she does not come through with her promises, she becomes very unpopular.

Brady Tidbit:
Cindy is missing her curls in this episode!!! Her hair is down for the first time in the series.

EPISODE #109: Kelly's Kid

Written: Sherwood Schwartz
Director: Richard Michaels
Airdate: January 4, 1974

Carol and Mike's good friends, the Kellys, are adopting an eight-year-old son, Matt. When Matt misses his friends from the orphanage, they adopt his other two friends.

Brady Tidbit:

This episode was written by Sherwood Schwartz himself in hopes that this show would be a spin-off to the Bradys. Even though the show was never picked up, in 1986 it was finally made as *Together We Stand*, starring Elliott Gould and Dee Wallace and produced only thirteen episodes.

Brady House Guest:

Ken Berry "Ken Kelly"
Berry was best known for his role as Sam Jones on *The Andy Griffin Show*, then later in *Mayberry R.F.D.* and *Mama's Family*.
Brooke Bundy "Kathy Kelly"
Bundy appeared in two *Nightmare on Elm Street* movies and also guest-starred on *Charlie's Angels*, *Wonder Woman*, *Matlock*, and *Moonlighting*, among others.
Todd Lookinland "Matt Kelly"
Lookinland plays the newly-adopted son of the Kellys. Lookinland is the brother of Mike Lookinland.

Episode #110: The Driver's Seat
Written: George Tibbles
Director: Jack Arnold
Airdate: January 11, 1974
Jan is on the debate team and has to be replaced after she freezes. Marcia, too, freezes during her driving test. They both overcome their fears and are successful.

Bradywood:
Greg mentions that Marcia is funnier than Lucille Ball. At the time, Lucille Ball was filming her show *Here's Lucy* on the Paramount lot.

Episode #111: Out of this World
Written: Al Schwartz & Larry Rhine
Director: Peter Baldwin
Airdate: January 18, 1974
Peter and Bobby think they see a UFO, but no one believes them so they camp out to collect evidence. Bobby dreams that aliens come to earth, but it's Greg who is playing the real alien trick on them.

Brady Tidbit:
Barry Williams sports a cut lip in this episode which was to cover the real-life auto accident he had which he needed stitches.
The two actors playing the aliens were Cindy's, Peter's, Jan's, and Bobby's stand-ins for the series.

Brady House Guest:
Brigadier General James A. McDivitt "Himself"
McDivitt was the Commander of the Gemini 4 space walk and Apollo 9 space mission.

Episode #112: Welcome Aboard
Written: Larry Rhine & Al Schwartz
Director: Richard Michaels
Airdate: January 24, 1974
Cousin Oliver is moving in. Yet where Cousin Oliver goes disaster follows and he overhears the kids complaining about him. His luck changes when he becomes the family's lucky ninth member and wins the family guest extras parts in a movie.

Brady Tidbit;
Robert Rist was brought in as Cousin Oliver in an attempt to keep the young audience.
The Bradys visit a studio, Marathon Studios, which was really Paramount, where they shot *The Brady Bunch*.

Episode #113: Two Pete's in the Pod
Written: Sam Locke & Milton Pascal
Director: Richard Michaels
Airdate: February 8, 1974
Peter runs into Arthur Owens at school who is a dead ringer for him. Peter has two dates and asks Arthur to take one of them. Date night gets complicated when both dates arrive early.

Brady Tidbit:
Peter mentions that Cindy, Bobby and Cousin Oliver are worse than Jesse James who was Bobby's idol in "Bobby's Hero" (#89).

Brady House Guest:
Christopher Knight "Arthur Owens"
He plays a twin boy who just moved to town.

OMB!:
One would think if you had a twin who lived in the same town you would become friends and just maybe have a question or two for your mother?

Ten ways you know you're as perfect as Marcia

1. You brush your hair 100 times per night.
2. Can't help being as popular as you are.
3. Being so humble about being so popular.
4. Dating as many boys at one time and you just can't decide.
5. Being an ultra-safe driver.
6. You stand up for the rights of others.
7. Having pure self-confidence with yourself
8. Having to buy a new shelf for all your trophies.
9. You know all the grooviest words to say.
10. Just because she's Marcia!

Episode #114: Top Secret

Written: Howard Ostroff
Director: Bernard Wiesen
Airdate: February 15, 1974
Cousin Oliver and Bobby figure Mike is working undercover with the FBI and figure Sam "the butcher" is a double agent.

Episode #115: The Snooperstar
Written: Harry Winkler
Director: Bruce Bilson
Airdate: February 22, 1974
Cindy feels something is going on and reads Marcia's diary. Marcia finds out she is reading her diary and sets Cindy up with a fake entry that mentions she will be the new Shirley Temple.

Brady House Guest:
Natalie Schafer "Penelope Fletcher"
Schafer plays the wealthy client of Mike Brady. Schafer is best known for playing Lovey Howell on *Gilligan's Island*.

Episode #116: The Hustler
Written: Bill Freedman & Ben Gershman
Director: Michael J. Kane
Airdate: March 1, 1974
Mike is sent a pool table by the president of his company. Bobby is an excellent pool player and then bets Mike's boss and wins.

Brady House Guest:
Jim Backus "Harry Matthews"
Backus plays the President of Mike's office. Backus is best known for his work as Thurston Howell III on *Gilligan's Island* and was also the voice of Mr. Magoo. He was also in two other Brady episodes, "Grand Canyon or Bust" (#50) and "Ghost Town USA" (#51).

Episode #117: The HairBrained Scheme

Written: Charles Stewart, Jr.
Director: Jack Arnold
Airdate: March 8, 1974
Bobby starts selling hair tonic to make a million dollars. When Greg buys a bottle, his hair turns orange – and his graduation is tomorrow!

Brady Tidbit:
Robert Reed hated this script so much he refused to work on this episode. This is the final episode of the series.

Brady House Guest:
Hope Schwartz plays "Gretchen"

Eve Plumb, who was Jan Brady, is now known for her paintings.
(photo courtesy Chris Haston)

The Brady Toy Chest & Record Set

Here is a list of the classic toy items that came out on *The Brady Bunch* in the 1970s. The list also includes the record and tracks the Brady Kids released. Most of their music, which was out on vinyl, is now on CD or on iTunes for purchase!

Brady toys

Books
The Brady Bunch by William Johnston 1969
The Brady Bunch: Showdown at the PTA Corral by William Johnston 1969
The Brady Bunch: Count Up to Blast Down by William Johnston 1969
The Brady Bunch: The Bumbler by William Johnston 1970
The Brady Bunch: The Quarterback Who Came to Dinner by William Johnston 1970
The Brady Bunch: The Treasure of Mystery Island by Jack Matcha 1972
The Brady Bunch: The New York Mystery by Jack Matcha 1972
The Bardy Bunch: Adventure on the High Seas by Jack Matcha 1972

Coloring/Activity books
The Brady Bunch Coloring Book #1035 1972 published by Whitman Publishing
The Brady Bunch Coloring Book #1061 1973 published by Whitman Publishing
The Brady Bunch Coloring Book #1004 1974 published by Whitman Publishing
The Brady Bunch Activity Book 1974 published by Larami

Comic Books
#1: The Brady Bunch: Here Comes the Brady Bunch 1970 by Dell
#2: The Brady Bunch: Why Parent Get Gray or 3+3=Too Much 1970 by Dell

Various Items
The Brady Bunch Lunchbox with Thermos 1970
The Brady Bunch Topps Trading Cards
    1971 release 88-card set
    1970 release 55-card set
1972-1973 Whitman/Western Publishing released four different Paper Dolls sets.
"The Grand Canyon Adventure" Viewmaster by GAF Corporation, 1971
    Released 3-reels with a booklet non-talking
    Released Gift Pack with talking
The Brady Bunch Board Game - 1973 - Whitman Publishing
Brady Bunch Tray Puzzle - Whitman 1972
Halloween Costumes - Greg & Marcia Brady
Brady Bunch variety items by Larami 1973
    Larami produced many different items which showcased different items of the Bradys, such as Tambourine, Banjo, Guitar Magic Slate, Chess Set, Hex-a-game, Twister, Tea Set, Supermarket Grocery set.

Fan Club Kit - Tiger Beat - 1972

    Tiger Beat was a leader on teen stars. They produced many magazines on the series stars and this fan kit, which included a record, autographs photos, membership card and wallet photos.

groovy tip!
One of the strangest things made with the Bradys on it are cigar bands from England! Smoke them if you got them, Greg!

Brady records
Merry Christmas from the Brady Bunch -1970 - Paramount Records/ Famous Music
Meet the Brady Bunch - 1972 - Paramount Records/Famous Music
Kids from the Brady Bunch 1972 - Paramount Records/Famous Music
Chris Knight and Maureen McCormick - 1973 - Paramount Records/ Famous Music
The Brady Bunch Photographic Album 1973 - Paramount Records/Famous Music
It's a Sunshine Day: The Best of the Brady Bunch 1993 - CD by Juicemaster & MCA

The New Brady Dolls
Classic TV Toys recently produced new Brady dolls. The dolls are eight inches and come dressed in a colorful jumpsuit and come in Carol, Marsha, Jan, Cindy, Greg, Peter, Bobby and Alice. The dolls are available at www.ClassicTVToys.com. Owner Steve Sandberg gave us some insight about the dolls:

Why the Bradys?
We had looked at some of the classic licenses form the '60s &'70s. We thought it was a retro doll for adults and the next generation for kids. We thought it would be a pretty nice license to bring back.

Did you work with the actors?
No, just with Paramount Pictures.

Was there a reason you didn't do a Mike Brady doll?
His estate chose not have anything to do with going forward with a license.

Which doll sells best?
Marcia is very popular and sold very well.

Were you a fan of the show?
I like the show and I thought the show tried to, given the time period, capture the moment.

**The Brady's
4222 Clinton Way!
555-6161**

Come By and have a Sunshinny Day!

Bibliography

Williams, Barry and Kreski, Chris. *Growing Up Brady: I Was a Teenage Greg*, HarperPerennial; 1992

Stoddard, Sylvia. *TV Treasures a Companion Guide to the Brady Bunch*, St. Martin's Paperbacks; 1996

Foreverbrady.com, www.foreverbrady.com

The Internet Movie Database, www.imdb.com, Brady Bunch page.

Wikipedia.com, Brady Bunch page.

Brady Bunch Season One (DVD); Featurette: "The Brady Bunch – Coming Together Under One Roof" Paramount Pictures 2005

The Brady Home Movies (DVD); Rhino Home Video, 2000.

Bradymania: A Very Brady Special; The Learning Channel, 2000.

Thank You!

Special Thank you to Susan Olsen, who took time out of her busy life! You're the best!

Sweet thank you to Ann B. Davis, who took the time to chat about the world's favorite housekeeper, Alice! You could boil me water anytime!

A heartfelt thank you to Sherwood Schwartz. It was so amazing to chat with you about the Bradys. Thank you, thank you, thank you!!

Lloyd Schwartz, thank you for taking time to chat with me about everything Brady!

Geri Reischl, my favorite Jan! It was wonderful to meet you and have you be a part of my project.

Hope Juber, you were so sweet to chat with me about your Brady memories! It was so nice to chat.

Rob Rist, it was super-fun chatting with you about Cousin Oliver!!!

Thank you to Zach Bostrom for sharing with me your life as an extended Brady!

An ultra-special thank-you to all the Brady Bunch cast: without you, there would be no Bradyisms!!! Robert Reed, Florence Henderson, Barry Williams, Maureen McCormick, Christopher Knight, Eve Plumb and Mike Lookinland

Thank you to Wendy Winans, of **BradyWorld.com,** with chatting with me and creating the best Brady website online!!

Ted Nichelson, thank you for everything - you're a true BRADY!!!

Many kisses to my mom and dad! Thanks again for being such special people who support me in everything I do! I love you both so much.

Thank you to my friends: Vanessa Guild, Monica Holmes, Scott Jonson, Chris Kosloski, Brian Lamberson, Ellen Loughin, Jules Massey, Joey Marshall, **Shaun Neale,** Michael Now, Eric Thomson, Skip O'Brien, Sean Olson, Dawn Robinson, Morgan Slate, Charlene Tilton.

Once again, thank you, Farrah Fawcett and Cheryl Ladd, you are both true angels to me!

Charlene Tilton thanks for doing my foreword for the book and being such a great friend always! Love you always!

A HUGE thank you to Michael Derry for you're brilliant and wonderful character artwork of The Bradys. It's so Michael, Michael, Michael!!! Thanks!

A very colorful Thank You to Julian Roca, Danielle Buerli, David Prosenko and everyone over at ArtMachine for making my book cover so GROOVY!

..and thank you to Ben Ohmart, Darlene Swanson and everyone over at BearManor for their hard work on my newest book. It has been a great pleasure to work with all of you again!

...to my sister and her family, who this book is dedicated to.

About the artist
Michael Derry
Creator of *The Brady Bunch* artwork.

Michael Derry started drawing before he could remember and won his first art contest in kindergarten at the tender age of five. It was for a fire prevention poster. The medium was Crayola and if you want to see it, you'll have to ask his mother.

He graduated from Northern Illinois University in DeKalb with a BFA in Illustration. In 1998 he has been writing and drawing his comic strip *Troy*, which appears in print and on the web throughout the US, Canada, the UK, South Africa, parts of South America, and Australia.

In 2008, he had his first solo show, "Groovy, Silly, Sexy, Cute," at Grace Ellay in Los Angeles. "Groovy…" included several pieces featuring the boys of *Troy*, his fabulous, voluptuous Derry Products girls, as well as several other illustrations and paintings. More on Derry at www.derry-products.com or www.troycomics.com.

Mike Pingel with Greg Brady & Mama Brady, Marsh!

About the Author

Mike Pingel, writer, actor, and publicist, graduated from American University in Washington, D.C.

Pingel's passion for the TV series *Charlie's Angels* led him into creating the website www.charliesangels.com, then running Cheryl Ladd's official website. This was followed by being hired as Farrah Fawcett's personal assistant in 2005.

He has written three books, *Angelic Heaven: The Fan's Guide to Charlie's Angels*, *The Q Guide to Charlie's Angels*, and *The Q Guide to Wonder Woman*.

Most recently, Pingel made guest appearances in the *Chico's Angels* series, Marc Anthony's music video, "Ahora Quien," and Farrah's reality series, *Chasing Farrah*.

Pingel owns/operates several websites, including the entertainment website, www.hollywoodFYI.com.

For up-to-date information on Pingel, please visit his website at www.MikePingel.com.